PENGUIN BOOKS

WOMEN AND CHILL

Ruth Sidel is a graduate of Wellesley College and the Boston University School of Social Work. She has helped emotionally disturbed preschool children for several years and, most recently, has been Social Work Supervisor at the Comprehensive Child Care Project associated with the Albert Einstein College of Medicine. Since her return from China, she has lectured extensively on her trip. Mrs. Sidel lives in Riverdale, New York, with her husband, Victor W. Sidel, and her two sons, Mark and Kevin.

RUTH SIDEL

WOMEN AND CHILD CARE IN CHINA

A FIRSTHAND REPORT

PHOTOGRAPHS BY VICTOR W. SIDEL

Penguin Books Inc
Baltimore • Maryland

Penguin Books Inc
7110 Ambassador Road
Baltimore, Maryland 21207, U.S.A.

First published by Hill and Wang, a division of
Farrar, Straus and Giroux, New York, 1972

Published in Penguin Books 1973
Reprinted 1974

Printed in the United States of America by
Murray Printing Co., Forge Village, Massachusetts

To Vic, Mark, and Kevin,

with love

To our Chinese hosts,

with thanks

ACKNOWLEDGMENTS

Our thanks, first, to Arthur Galston, Professor of Biology at Yale University. He and Ethan Signer, of M.I.T., spent two and a half weeks in China in the spring of 1971, thereby becoming the first American scientists to visit the People's Republic of China in over twenty years. Dr. Galston's letter on behalf of my husband and myself to Dr. Kuo Mo-jo, president of the Chinese Academy of Sciences, was of primary importance in our receiving an invitation to spend a month in China as the guests of the Chinese Medical Association.

We are grateful to the Chinese Medical Association for its kind invitation and magnificent hospitality. We were accompanied throughout our trip by Comrade Hsu Shou-jen, secretary general of the Chinese Medical Association, an indefatigable host with a twinkle in his eye; Mr. Kan Hsing-fa, an excellent interpreter; and Dr. Hsu Chia-yu, our primary interpreter, who is deputy head of the Department of Internal Medicine at the East Is Red (Dong Fang Hong) Hospital in Shanghai. Dr. Hsu was a warm, generous, and gracious host who spared no effort to help us understand his country and make us comfortable. We thank them all for a wonderful experience.

I owe special thanks to Janie and Richard Kaplan, who stayed with our two sons for the month we were away; to Ruth Freed, who read the manuscript and made countless valuable suggestions; to Mary Schroepfer, who typed the manuscript; and to Henry Chin, who translated the children's reader in the appendix. Also my gratitude to Livia Cersosimo, Flora Donham, Brina Melemed, our sons Kevin and Mark, Lili Soohoo, and Mary Ellen and Arthur Wang.

Above all, I should like to thank my husband, who contributed not only the photographs but limitless help and encouragement.

CONTENTS

INTRODUCTION

During the two weeks from the day we received our invitation to visit China until we left New York, I thought about the aspects of life in China I should observe. I wanted to experience the feel and rhythm of the country, become acquainted with some of its people, and learn about its goals and how the country was trying to achieve them. But I know that one learns substantially more about a country if one can explore one facet in some depth.

As a psychiatric social worker, I have worked with emotionally disturbed pre-school children and their families. In my most recent position in a pediatric health center, I worked with families with physical, emotional, and environmental problems. I have also for some time been interested in day care for the pre-school child and have visited day-care centers in the Soviet Union, Scandinavia, and England. My interest in day care has included its potential effect on children. And, as a working mother, I have been concerned about the growing American problem of arranging for the care of young children in order to free mothers to do what the Chinese call "productive labor." Care for the small child must be provided, of course, if women in our society are to develop their potential and make their maximum contribution. During our stay in China, therefore, I decided to try to learn as much as I could about the interrelated role of women and the care of pre-school children.

My husband is chief of the Department of Social Medicine at Montefiore Hospital in the Bronx, New York, and is particularly concerned with medical care, the training of medical personnel, and medical problems that are related to environmental problems. He has studied medical care in the Soviet Union, Scandinavia, and Great Britain and was interested in looking at the Chinese system of urban medical care and the kinds of medical personnel China is training.

While in China, we visited medical schools, hospitals, neighborhood health stations, factories, communes, child-care centers, and places of historical interest. We visited three nursing rooms, four nurseries (and heard in detail about a fifth), and seven kindergartens. My husband and I made these visits together, one of us taking pictures while the other took notes. We were free to wander anywhere and spent many hours walking the streets of Peking, Shanghai, Canton, and Hangchow. We were free to take pictures except at the airports, which serve military as well as civilian purposes, and at the border. We took 1,700 pictures.

We expected to see a poor country with some of the usual signs of poverty—teeming cities with beggars in the streets. We expected to see a country with a strong military presence, marching men, and a highly visible army. And we expected to see and be alienated by a strong Mao cult whose central purpose is the glorification of the Chairman.

What we found was a poor country without beggars. People go about their daily work with a purpose and even a sense of mission. It is a country where the basic necessities are provided but in which there are still few material conveniences and people work very hard, particularly in the countryside. China does have a large urban population, 150 million, probably the largest urban population in the world, but 80 percent of the population—650 million—lives in the countryside and one's overall impression is of a rural country, green, quiet, and heavily planted.

The army is present everywhere, but as members of revolutionary committees of all the institutions of the society; we never saw the military march at all. And Mao is everywhere. But we came to feel that his pictures, statues, quotes, and poems are there not simply to glorify a leader but to teach a system of values as well.

Much of this book may sound unduly optimistic; people may seem unbelievably happy; there may seem to be a striking lack of conflict. I would like to offer several explanations for the seeming happiness and joy. First and of prime importance, the Chinese compare their present life not to life in other societies but to life in the "bitter past," prior to the revolution in 1949—and, in comparison, life does seem fine indeed. Second, the matters on which we concentrated—the role of women, the care of children, and medicine—are those in which the Chinese have made astonishing progress, and they are justifiably proud of their accomplishments.

In addition, as Marc Riboud has observed, the Chinese tend to describe conditions as they wish them to be, not always as they are. And, of course, we were guests, American guests at that. And one is unlikely to tell one's troubles to foreign guests. There is clearly more conflict and dissension in China than we could possibly see. Moreover, we speak no Chinese; even with our excellent interpreter, we were at a disadvantage and surely missed many nuances of meaning. I have, however, tried to describe the Chinese as we saw them, using direct quotes whenever possible. Too, we were in China a brief time, just about a month. We saw only a little of that vast country.

Our itinerary, briefly, was as follows: We flew from New York to Hong Kong and then took the train to the border. After passing through passport control and having our first of many delicious meals, we proceeded by train to Canton, where we spent three days. We then flew to Peking, where we stayed for ten days. We were at the Peking Hotel, a large, lively hotel down the street from Tien An Men Square (the Gate of Heavenly Peace). We flew to Shanghai, stayed one week at the pre-war Peace Hotel, whose dining room provided delicious food and a magnificent view of the Hwang Pu River, and then took the train to Hangchow, where we spent three days in a modern guest house overlooking the beautiful West Lake. We flew from Hangchow back to Canton and the next morning took the train back to the border.

The Chinese have been grappling with many of the problems we in the West are concerned with—equality for women, the care of children, the communication of a system of values from one generation to another. Perhaps some of their experiences can enlighten our search for solutions.

1

A Brief Look
at the "Bitter Past"

The mother-in-law, showing the effects of a hard life, was little more than a living corpse, so Gold Flower did not suffer much from that quarter as did most Chinese brides. But her husband made up for this lack, treating her worse than a dozen mothers-in-law. She had to wait on him, day and night. When he went to sleep she had to take off his shoes and clothing; in the morning, she had to put them on again. She had to light his cigarettes, pour his water, hand him the cup with both hands and with a subservient smile on her face. He struck her daily as a matter of course and beat her unmercifully if she did not obey his commands on the instant.

JACK BELDEN
Gold Flower's Story, in
China Shakes the World

THE CHINESE TODAY RARELY SPEAK OF THE past; they speak only of the "bitter past." When remembering and recounting events going back before 1949, before the "Liberation" of the mainland by the Communists, they refer to the "bitter past" when starvation, disease, and oppression were a way of life for millions of Chinese people, both urban and rural. The Chinese peasant, who comprises the vast majority of the population, lived under a dual system of oppression, a semifeudal economic system and the traditional family. Both were based on a hierarchy of domination and subservience which was enforced at all levels with brutality and violence. As William Hinton in his book *Fanshen* describes it: "Husbands beat their wives, mothers-in-laws beat their daughters-in-law, peasants beat their children, landlords beat their tenants, and the Peace Preservation Corps beat anyone who got in the way." [1] Although traditional family and village life contained elements of mutual caring, there was omnipresent exploitation—by the government, the war lords, landlords, husbands, and mothers-in-law—of the peasant, his wife, and their children. Traditionally, landlords or rich peasants, who comprised approximately 10 percent

[1] William Hinton: *Fanshen* (New York: Vintage Books, 1966), p. 51.

3

of the population and owned 55 to 65 percent of the land, rented small segments to the peasants to farm.[2] The peasants did not pay rent in cash but paid from 50 to as much as 80 or 90 percent of their harvest. If, because of drought or flood, sickness or other disaster, a peasant was unable to pay the landlord, he could take out a loan either in grain or in money from the landlord, now acting in the capacity of usurer. If he then could not repay the loan, he could be forced off the land by the landlord. The peasant would thus be deprived of any way of earning a living or feeding his family; his family might well starve to death.

In reviewing the history of the village of Long Bow in Shansi Province in the early 1940's, Hinton describes Sheng Ching-ho, the richest landlord in the village, and his financial dealings with some of the Long Bow peasants. He would lend money to the peasants, charging as much as 50 percent interest a month, and when they could not pay, would confiscate their land, their livestock, their carts, and their implements, with dire results for the peasants.

Hang-sheng was an old man who owned half an acre of very good land just to the east of the village. In a crisis he once borrowed $13 from Sheng Ching-ho. Three years later the principal plus interest amounted to a very large sum. Though Hang-Sheng paid off some of it, he couldn't pay it all. Ching-ho then seized the half acre and the summer harvest that had just been reaped on it. Because he did not want the millet he plowed it under and planted wheat in the fall. Hang-sheng was left with nothing.

[2] Jack Belden: *China Shakes the World* (New York: Monthly Review Press, 1949), p. 149.

A poor peasant named Shen borrowed $4 from Ching-ho in order to buy medicine for his sick wife. As a guarantee for the loan he indentured his son Fa-liang to Ching-ho for seven years. At the end of seven years, because of illness, deductions for broken tools, and outright cheating on the part of Ching-ho, Fa-liang owed many times the original debt and had to tear down part of his house and sell the roof timbers to win his freedom.[3]

Not only did the landlord have complete control over the peasants because of the economic framework, but his authority extended to the peasant's wife and daughters as well. Jack Belden, who in *China Shakes the World* has given a first-hand account of conditions in China in the late 1940's, reports:

The power of the landlords gave them control over village women, especially the wives of their tenants, with whom they could have whatever relations pleased them. Very often, the tenant and his wife acquiesced in these relations out of fear but if the tenant should protest, he had little chance to make his protest effective. In a village in western Shantung I came across a landlord whose common practice was to make his tenant go out into the field and work while he took his pleasure of the tenant's wife. When Li protested, the landlord had him kidnapped by bandits. In order to cover his participation in the kidnapping, the landlord pretended to mediate the affair through puppet troops, preparing a banquet on the tenant's behalf. But observe the cleverness of this plot. The grateful tenant was released and borrowed money from the kindly landlord to pay for the banquet. Of course, a

[3] Hinton, pp. 30–33.

high interest rate was charged, the tenant could not repay his debt, and lost his own small plot of ground. The landlord then consummated the whole affair by taking the tenant's wife as payment of the debt.[4]

The landlords, however, did not need to be devious. When they wanted a woman, they would simply order her to submit, or rape her outright. There was little the peasants could do.

The family life of both peasants and gentry was governed as well by a highly structured authoritarian system. All family members had their place "in proper order by their age," and respect for the older members, chronologically and in generation, was a basic principle of life. The kinship system was based on three factors: generation, age, and proximity of kinship. One's place in the system was determined and fixed.

Family relations were based on the "six kinship relations," called Liu Ch'in, which traditionally delimited the extended family. The "six kinship relations" were between: (1) husband and wife; (2) husband and children; (3) brothers; (4) the children of brothers; (5) the brothers' grandchildren; and (6) the brothers' great-grandchildren. The first four of these kinship relations determined the size of the extended family; the last two enlarged it to a clan.[5]

Relationships between parents and children were based on the dual principles of filial piety and veneration of age. In his study, "The Chinese Family in the Communist Revolution," C. K. Yang tells us: "Filial piety demanded absolute obedience and complete devotion to the parents, thus establishing the generational

[4] Belden, p. 155.
[5] C. K. Yang: "The Chinese Family in the Communist Revolution," in *Chinese Communist Society: The Family and the Village* (Cambridge, Mass.: M.I.T. Press, 1965), p. 8.

subordination of the children." [6] As the peasants were completely subservient to the landlords, so were the children completely subservient to the parents. Filial piety was enhanced by genuine affection between parents and their children, and these emotional bonds were further strengthened by the mutual interdependence of parents and children. Parents were dependent on their sons for security in their old age; children were dependent on their parents for survival. The existence of children was threatened from all sides. Infanticide was legal; physical abuse was rife; and the peasants were powerless to assure the basic necessities. Here are two of the stories told to William Hinton:

> There were three famine years in a row. The whole family went out to beg things to eat. In Chinchang City conditions were very bad. Many mothers threw new-born children into the river. Many children wandered about on the streets and couldn't find their parents. We had to sell our eldest daughter. She was then already 14. Better to move than to die, we thought. We sold what few things we had. We took our patched quilt on a carrying pole and set out for Changchin with the little boy in the basket on the other end. Because the boy wept so bitterly a woman came out. We stayed there three days. On the fourth morning the woman said she wanted to buy the boy. We put him on the k'ang. He fell asleep. In the next room we were paid five silver dollars. Then they drove us out. They were afraid when the boy woke up he would cry for his mother. My heart was so bitter. To sell one's own child was such a painful thing. We wept all day on the road.

> During the famine we ate leaves and the remnants from vinegar making. We were so weak and hungry

6 Ibid., p. 89.

we couldn't walk. I went out to the hills to get leaves and there the people were fighting each other over the leaves on the trees. My little sister starved to death. My brother's wife couldn't bear the hunger and ran away and never came back. My cousin was forced to become a landlord's concubine.[7]

When one thinks of the traditional Chinese family, one thinks of hundreds of thousands of family units across the face of China all functioning in a similar way. Class distinctions, however, introduced important differences in family organization. The Western view of a large clan living together and taking responsibility for one another in strict adherence to the kinship system is basically the Confucian ideal and was more prevalent in the upper classes than among the peasants. Some of the customs of the upper classes—such as foot-binding —were passed on to the peasants and assimilated by them; but economic necessity modified these for the peasants.

One theory suggests that where women participated in production, they had some power. Peasant women toiled in the fields or cared for the livestock; this gave them the advantage of participating in policy-making within their families—which women of the upper class did not have. Upper-middle-class women had the least power, for in the families of landlords and gentry the men had ample time to take care of family affairs, and women did no productive work. These families exercised great cruelty toward the lower classes, including buying and selling of servants; as an integral part of marriage, concubines were maintained and prostitutes frequented. It was in middle-class families that women,

[7] Hinton, pp. 42–43.

both the wives and socially inferior women, were most exploited.

In the upper classes in traditional China the men were occupied with their own affairs to such an extent that the women had great influence in the raising of the children and played a larger role in family affairs. In the first half of the twentieth century, a select group of upper-class women managed to obtain a university education and some went on to become doctors, scientists, and educators. In 1934, 15 percent of the students in institutions of higher education were women. The most popular field for them was education, followed by literature and the arts, science, and health. By 1946 the number of women studying at universities in China had risen to 18 percent, and nearly one-third of these women went into education. By 1946, 28 percent were studying to enter the health professions.[8] The involvement of women in the health field began as early as the 1890's, when a small number of women studied in the United States under missionary auspices. In spite of the hostility women entering medicine might be expected to arouse, women doctors had successful careers, because of the traditional reluctance of Chinese women to be examined by male physicians.

With the rise of the feminist movement during the second and third decades of the century, a few noted women became politically influential. Three women—Madame Sun Yat-sen, Madame Liao Chung-kai, and Madame Wang Ching-wei—were elected in 1924 to the first Congress of the Kuomintang. Madame Liao remained active in government and in 1949 was appointed by the Communists Director of the Commis-

[8] Leo A. Orleans: *Professional Manpower and Education in Communist China,* The Library of Congress, p. 172.

sion of Overseas Chinese Affairs. Madame Sun Yat-sen, otherwise known as Soong Ching Ling, was one of the founders of the China Welfare Federation in 1938 and is today a Deputy Chairman of the People's Republic of China. Other women as well made an impact on pre-revolutionary China. But they were the exceptions to the general status of women before 1949.

In the decades preceding Liberation, the nuclear family was small. Indications are that the average family in nine counties of Szechwan Province in 1942–43 consisted of 4.4 to 5.3 persons. In another study of twenty-three provinces, the average family ranged from 4.1 persons in Jehol Province to 5.9 persons in Anhwei Province.[9] Hinton reports that, in the village of Long Bow, family size was directly related to class. "The landlords and the rich peasants averaged more than five persons per household, the middle peasants fewer than five, the poor peasants between three and three and a half, and the hired laborers about three."[10] The smallness of the peasant family was in part due to the high rate of infant and child mortality. Whenever economically feasible, however, the married son, his wife, and their children lived with the paternal grandparents, thus constituting an enlarged extended family. The higher the class standing of the family, the larger the number of people who lived together. Han Suyin, who has written extensively about life in China both prior to and since Liberation, tells that seventy-five people, excluding servants, lived in her grandmother's house in the last decade of the nineteenth century. She quotes her father's description of their upper-middle-class family life in Szechwan at that time:

[9] Yang, pp. 7–8.
[10] Hinton, p. 28.

There was, in the complex of relationships in which we lived, a pyramid of authority, not only of people, but of rooms and courtyards, trees and flowers, servants and sedan chairs. My father and my mother were always completely dressed as if for an official call when visiting my grandfather in his room in the same house. Awesome in dignity, he granted us, his grandchildren, a morning audience of ten minutes; we changed our clothes, washed our face and hands to bow to him and wish him good day.[11]

The superior position of the male in pre-Liberation China is evident. The purpose of marriage was to produce male heirs to perpetuate the paternal grandparents' family, to assure the continuity of the husband's family structure, and to provide additional work power, from the son- and daughter-in-law. The preference for male children, the importance of descendants through the male line, and the young wife's moving in with the paternal inlaws are further evidences of male dominance. Peasants were oppressed by poverty, the threat of starvation, and their subservience to the landlord; the women suffered, in addition, the domination of the males and the older females in the family. Before 1949, women were worse than second-class citizens; they were very nearly slaves. Let us look at what the life of a girl from a peasant family might have been like in pre-Communist Chinese society.

If one was unfortunate enough to be born female, before 1949, one might very well not survive. Female babies were an economic liability; they would never become part of the family's work force and would only bring a marriage price. Often, parents did not know

[11] Han Suyin: *The Crippled Tree* (New York: G. P. Putnam's Sons, 1965), p. 75.

how they could feed a daughter, and, in fact, the practice of drowning girl babies was common. Those female babies that survived were likely to be treated warmly and permissively the first few years. Between the ages of five and seven they might have their feet tightly bound, so that, in the future, walking would be nearly impossible.

Foot-binding,[12] a practice that continued well into the 1940's though it was officially banned in 1911, was apparently started in the courts of the Southern T'ang Dynasty in A.D. 937 when the Emperor had a six-foot lotus fashioned out of gold and decorated with jewels for his court dancer. He "ordered the maiden to bind her feet with white silk cloth to make the tips look like the points of the moon sickle. She then danced in the center of the golden lotus with tiptoe steps, whirling about like a rising cloud, and the effect was so pleasing to the Emperor that he called the bound foot of his dancer 'Golden Lotus' (Chin Lien)." Other court dancers, too, bound their feet; and eventually the foot was bound so tightly that not only was dancing impossible but walking became extremely difficult. The feet of young girls were bound after first being soaked in hot water, then massaged; the four toes were flexed and pressed over the sole of the foot and bandaged with a cloth two inches wide and ten feet long. Suffering great pain, the young girl was made to walk on the bound foot with a shoe on that was made progressively smaller until, after two or three years of having the bandages tightened, the foot was reduced to three and a half to

[12] Much of this material on foot-binding has been taken from Lily Mary Veronica Chan: "Foot Binding in Chinese Women and Its Psycho-social Implications," *Canadian Psychiatric Journal,* Vol. 15 (April 1970), pp. 229–31.

four inches. The bound foot "became a symbol of the subordinate role of women in China, and at the same time a mark of femininity and beauty . . ." In 1942, in the liberated areas, the Communists issued a proclamation abolishing foot-binding. But they found that simply issuing the order, and even fining the families of women with bound feet, was not effective; they then rescinded the order and instead educated the people about foot-binding. Gradually, the practice was abandoned.

In addition to having their feet bound, women were kept to their menial role by a number of other practices. Illiteracy was generally high in China before Liberation, and women were denied an education even more systematically than men. Pre-school education did not exist prior to Liberation. With regard to primary schools, one source reports 24 million students attending in 1949;[13] another source reports 2 million primary-school graduates in 1948–49.[14] Thus, roughly one-third of the eligible population in any given year was attending primary school, and approximately one-fifth was graduating after six years of primary school. In one village in South China in 1950, 65 percent of the men over the age of ten were literate, and only 8 percent of the women. In nine counties in Szechwan Province in 1942 and 1943, 48 percent of the men were literate, and only 19 percent of the women.[15] In addition to being denied education, women were discouraged from developing any skill outside of those related to the home or from working outside the home. Thus, they would be completely dependent economically on their husbands

[13] Yang, p. 171.
[14] Orleans, p. 32.
[15] Yang, p. 112.

and on their inlaws, no matter how badly they were treated.

In all the social classes, whether urban or rural, girls were married at a young age to men they were likely not to know beforehand; the marriages were arranged by both sets of parents, with a view to strengthening the family of the groom. Girls were generally married at the ages of fifteen to seventeen, and boys at sixteen to eighteen, but frequently girls were married even younger than that, often as children. The young bride belonged to her husband's family and was discouraged from even visiting her own family. Essentially, she lost her identity as a human being and was totally subservient to the needs and wishes of her new family. She was no longer known by her name but was addressed by a term denoting her position in the new family. She was the last to eat and ate the most inferior foods available to the family; the clothing she was given was inadequate, and often she was cold in the winter. She was beaten at will by her husband and by others in his family. Most of all, she was a slave to her mother-in-law, who, similarly enslaved for years by her mother-in-law, perpetuated the tradition. Because she knew no trade and had no means of support, she was in bondage to her husband and his family.

Women were married for life; divorce was not permitted them. Even if the husband were to die, remarriage was frowned upon, for the widow was still considered part of her husband's family. When her existence became intolerable, she was advised: "When you marry a chicken, stick with the chicken; when you marry a dog, stick with the dog." Suicide was the only way out of her miserable existence, and suicides were not uncommon in the old China. According to Yang: "In 1935, when statistics were grossly incomplete, 1,353 suicides were reported in 244 counties and in 22 provinces. Of this total, 351, or 26.0 percent, were caused by domestic discord or matrimonial difficulties, which constituted the largest single item among all causes of suicide in China (economic difficulties caused 341 cases, or 25.2 percent, of all suicides). Among the 351 cases of suicide caused by family conflict 253, or 72 percent, were women." [16]

K. S. Karol, in his book *China: The Other Communism,* tells the story of Madame Chang Chiu-hsiang, who was born in 1910 and lived with her family in the northwest. After floods had destroyed their village, she and her family went to Shensi Province, but the family could not get enough to eat and her father sold her to another peasant for thirty-three pounds of grain. When she was thirteen, her new "father" too was forced to sell her because of lack of food, this time as a bride to an officer. But since she was so young, her "father" helped her escape before the wedding night and she "took to the roads of Shensi as a beggar." Madame Chang describes other girls like herself roaming the countryside in search of shelter and food. Luckily, she came upon her adopted father and once again he sold her as a bride, this time to a tenant farmer. Life improved somewhat and in 1935 she gave birth to a daughter and five years later to a son. Soon disaster struck again, however—her husband was arrested by Kuomintang soldiers. They managed to escape to the hills, and when they learned that the soldiers had left the village, they returned, destitute once again. Madame Chang in 1943 was forced to sell her own eight-year-old daughter to a rich peasant for fifty yuan of cotton. [17]

[16] Ibid., p. 107.
[17] K. S. Karol: *China: The Other Communism* (New York: Hill and Wang, 1968), pp. 167–69.

Thus, if a female child escaped infanticide, she faced the hazards of being sold to another family as a daughter or as a child bride. Eventually, her lot might improve if she bore her husband a son. After her child-bearing years, she attained the position of mother-in-law, with its attendent domination over lower-placed members of the family. Her life had reached its zenith.

As one might expect, the "bitter past" was not transformed suddenly after Liberation in 1949. From the turn of the century until the Revolution of 1911, Western ideas of equality for women and a less authoritarian family structure gradually penetrated the Chinese intellectual community. In 1911, with the overthrow of the Emperor and the rise to power of Sun Yat-sen, women's right to education was promulgated, women were encouraged to marry voluntarily and to participate in government. Following the Republican revolution, the New Culture movement of 1917, which in turn led to the May 4 movement of 1919, encouraged greater questioning of the traditional family, asked for a new role for women in the family as well as in society in general, called for voluntary marriage and for greater freedom for young people. An indication of the direction the Chinese intellectuals were moving in is the fact that Ibsen's plays became very popular.

With the second revolution of the mid-1920's, women gained greater political power and, in fact, became political workers in both the Kuomintang and the Communist Party. In 1924 the Kuomintang Party called for sex equality in law, in economic matters, in education, and in society in general; from the 1920's on, sex equality was accepted by the urban intelligentsia. With increased industrialization in the 1920's, 1930's, and 1940's, some families began drifting to the cities, where greater economic opportunities existed for men and occasionally for women. As the men worked farther from home in the cities than they had in the countryside, the women had more say in child-rearing and in running the home. The Sino-Japanese War (1937–45) and the Civil War (1945–49) increased the number of separated families and the power wielded by women. With industrialization, employment opportunities for women opened up in factories, and women became economic assets and were accorded more respect.

During the years 1938–45, major changes were being made in the structure of the family in the liberated areas, the areas wrested from Japanese control by Mao's Eighth Route Army. Here women made the most progress in attaining equality and throwing off the oppression that characterized their role in the traditional family. The Communist Party and the Eighth Route Army were committed to the equality of women. As they entered a village in the 1940's, one of their first acts would be to organize a women's association—a process that is described vividly by Jack Belden in "Gold Flower's Story." [18] A cadre (political worker) would round up some of the women and tell them that they need no longer live under bondage, that they had a right to equality with men, that they had a right to eat as well as the men and should not be beaten by their inlaws. The women were reluctant to speak up or to become part of such an association, because they were afraid. But the cadre would encourage a few to meet together and to tell the stories of their lives. This was the beginning of the "Speak Bitterness" sessions that were so successful in getting the villages to rally behind the Eighth

[18] Belden, pp. 275–307.

Route Army. Encouraging the women to recall and re-count the horrors under which they had been living sparked their anger, which soon sprang to the surface, impelling them to renounce their former role. From accounts of the "Speak Bitterness" meetings, it is clear that the effect was electric not only upon the person telling her story but upon those who listened as well. Identifying with the victim, the listeners would realize what conditions they themselves had been living under, and their anger and sorrow came to the fore.

After Gold Flower tells her story and receives the shouted encouragement of other women in her village, she returns to her inlaws' home a changed person. She can no longer accept the humiliations meted out to her by her father-in-law, her mother-in-law, and her husband. She must force them to alter their treatment of her and takes steps to fashion a new place for herself in her family and in the community.

The cadres who led these sessions knew the effectiveness of speaking out in a group about one's wretchedness and used this method to awaken the women of rural China in the 1940's to revolutionize their own roles and to support the Communist Revolution. Women were among the most ardent supporters of the Communist Revolution before Liberation, and the "Speak Bitterness" meetings which led to the formation of the women's associations played a major part in this. The women then became activists for others, not satisfied until every member of the village had at least become aware of the oppression they lived in. From the Women's Day, March 8, 1924, when a rally was held in Canton under Communist auspices, until Liberation in 1949, organizing the women's movement had top priority in the Communist Party.

2

The Liberation of Women

In order to build a great Socialist Society, it is of the utmost importance to arouse the broad masses of women to join in productive activity. Men and women must receive equal pay for equal work in production. Genuine equality between the sexes can only be realized in the process of the Socialist transformation of society as a whole.

MAO TSE-TUNG, 1955

"WE ARE ALL MASTERS OF NEW CHINA!" CHEN
Hui-cheng, a staff member of the Canton branch of the
Chinese Medical Association, told me with fervor in
her voice: "Now women have equal rights; we have political rights and economic rights. Women used to have
a low position in society," she went on, "they used to
marry young, have babies and worry about how to run
a family and serve their husband. Now it is entirely different. Now our great ambition is to make revolution."
We wondered, are women now masters of new China?
Do they have equal rights, politically and economically?
Everywhere we went, we asked these questions and
were invariably answered in the affirmative—women
do have equal rights. Have conditions really changed
this much since 1949? Let us go back briefly to the time
of Liberation.

The abolition of the landlord system and the intro-
duction of "fanshen," the turning over of the land to
the peasants, greatly weakened the authority of the traditional Chinese family but did not eradicate the values
it represented. The Communists in their 1950 Marriage
Law, one of the first major laws of the new government,
abolished arranged marriages, outlawed paying any
price in money or goods for a wife, outlawed polygamy,
concubines, and child marriage, prohibited interference

in the remarriage of widows, and guaranteed the right of divorce to the wife as well as to the husband. There was a rash of divorces following the 1950 Marriage Law, and on September 29, 1951, *Renmin Ribao* (*People's Daily*) reported 21,433 divorce cases, 76.6 percent of which had been brought by women.[1]

After the promulgation of the new Marriage Law, the Communist government placed special emphasis in their campaigns on raising the literacy of women. In 1950 there were 170 literacy groups consisting of 9,000 women from the Shanghai textile factories, and in 1951 the cities of Darien and Port Arthur reported that 94.5 percent or 8,640 illiterate women workers were attending literacy classes. Classes were organized in the rural areas as well; in the coastal counties of Shantung Province, for instance, there were 597 literacy classes for women in 1949, and in 1950 there were 1,687 classes, involving 40,000 women.[2]

But the key factor in the liberation of women was work. In the mid-1950's, the system of work points was introduced into the rural cooperatives. Although a woman worked and earned points and was paid according to how much she worked, hard manual labor accrued more work points; therefore, men earned more points than women. Furthermore, remuneration was made to the family rather than to the individual, thereby maintaining the interdependence of family members. With the establishment of communes in 1958, women had their first real chance at equality. As William Brugger says in his article, "The Male (and Female) in Chinese Society":

[1] Yang, p. 71.
[2] Ibid., p. 115.

The original aim of the People's Commune Movement was to create in the countryside organic communities, each of which was at the same time a unit of production, administration, defense (militia) and education. Each community was to be self reliant to a high degree, and was to combine agriculture with light industry as far as possible. The eventual aim was to make peasants wage earners, with no distinction between manual and mental work and no economic distinction between the sexes.

To this end canteens, creches, kindergartens, and subsidiary village industries to employ the underemployed (many of them women) were set up. This was to provide the economic equality of the sexes which would lead to eventual social equality.[3]

Women now receive equal pay for equal work (although hard manual labor still merits more work points than lighter manual labor) and are, therefore, not dependent upon their families or their husbands as they once were. But the role of women is closely linked to the economy; when employment drops, women workers are the first to be laid off. Thus, the liberation of women is inextricably tied to the fluctuation of employment in China since 1949.

In 1962, because of a general increase in unemployment, large numbers of women lost their jobs and families resumed the traditional pattern of husband as breadwinner and wife tending to domestic chores. Much of this was changed during the Cultural Revolution and we were told in the fall of 1971 that 90 percent of the women work, including those in the coun-

[3] William Brugger: "The Male (and Female) in Chinese Society," *Impact of Science on Society*, UNESCO, Vol. XXI, No. 1 (1971), pp. 13–14.

Physician in textile factory, Peking

tryside. And they work at a multitude of jobs: as factory workers, police, doctors, teachers, nurses, airplane pilots, bus drivers, cadres (political workers), and as members of the People's Liberation Army. In medicine, they constitute nearly one half of all doctors. Today, over 50 percent of all medical students are women, but they have entered in larger numbers than men the fields of pediatrics, psychiatry, internal medicine, and obstetrics/gynecology. Almost all obstetricians are women. All midwives, of course, are women, and a substantial number of barefoot doctors are women. ("Barefoot doctors" are peasants who have been trained for a brief period of time, usually three months, to treat "minor illnesses and common diseases," to provide health education, to immunize and offer other preventive services, and to supervise environmental sanitation. Barefoot doctors spend roughly half their time doing medical work and half of it working in the fields of their commune. They are paid in the same manner as their fellow peasants; they receive no extra pay for doing medical work. However, medical students are often chosen from among barefoot doctors.)

All nursery and kindergarten teachers are women. There seems to be no effort to recruit men into fields in which they would be dealing with small children. And there seems to be no concern for breaking down the traditional sex roles in professions such as teaching and nursing, both of which are virtually all female. Since most families in China are whole, consisting of both mother and father, the Chinese may not feel it imperative to provide male role-models for young children outside the home. Dr. Hsu, our interpreter, and Mr. Hsu, the secretary general of the Chinese Medical Association, with whom we discussed this point, both felt that sex-determined job preferences were natural; after all, the sexes are different and might well wish to enter different fields. Interestingly, Dr. Hsu's wife and Mr. Hsu's wife are professionals—the former a physician, and the latter a researcher in a scientific institute.

On the other hand, traditionally male professions are now being opened to women. In several recent issues of

Scientist, Institute for Biological Products, Peking

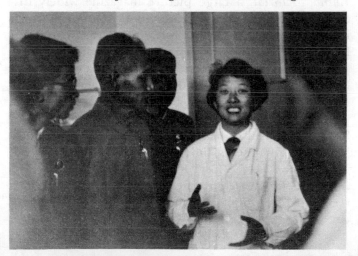

Boat-building on the Sing Sing Production Brigade, Shanghai

China Pictorial, a large picture magazine widely distributed in China which creates public opinion as much if not more than it reflects it, women were pictured as fruit pickers, textile workers, scientists, medical workers, welders, electrical workers, oil-well operators, vegetable growers, members of the militia, members of the Party Committee, printers, and members of the People's Liberation Army. Women are clearly pictured as "holding up half of heaven," as Mao has said.

Women, it appears, have acquired a great deal of political power at the local level. The society is divided into units which are governed by revolutionary committees. The revolutionary committees are, in turn, responsible at every level to party committees. A city is divided into districts, each district divided into streets, and each street divided into lanes; there is a revolutionary committee at each level.

For example, Hangchow, a beautiful green city about a hundred miles southwest of Shanghai, is built on the West Lake and has a population of 700,000. It is divided into four districts; one of these is divided into eight street committees. One particular street committee with a population of 7,350 families has twelve lanes; one of these lanes, Silvery Lane, consists of 702 families encompassing 2,700 people. The lane revolutionary committee, with nine members elected yearly, runs the primary school and the kindergarten, manages the local clothing factory, and administers the lane welfare fund. In general, the revolutionary committee of the lane is controlled by women—sometimes "housewives," sometimes retired workers living within the community. Every revolutionary committee is made up of what is known as the "Three-in-One-Combination"—that is, a representative of the People's Liberation Army, a cadre, and representatives elected from the "mass." The "mass" are members of any given organization such as medical workers in a hospital or all the residents in a given neighborhood.

Silvery Lane operates a health center whose director is a "housewife," an elderly, leathery-faced woman with deep wrinkles. She is a cadre and the chairman of the lane revolutionary committee; she works full-time at three jobs but receives no pay. Working under her in the health center are cadres and health workers, nearly all of whom are women. The health center and the work it does are an intimate part of the urban organization and these women clearly have a great deal of power in the neighborhoods within which they work. It has been suggested that the power of women at the local level is so great that it is responsible for the wiping out of prostitution in China since 1949 and for the tone of puritanism which pervades the cities.

Another example of the political power of urban women is the administration of a "workers' village," Chao Yang, in Shanghai. Chao Yang with its population of 68,000 (15,000 families) is a community built to house workers from the local textile factory. Within the community is a post office, a bank, a library, a cinema, a cultural station, a health station, barbershops, tailor shops, repair shops, restaurants, public baths, public gardens, and a swimming pool. Chao Yang has seven nurseries and kindergartens, fourteen primary schools, and seven middle schools. It is divided into eight lanes, each of which has a health clinic, a branch department store, and markets for vegetables, meats, and fruits.

The governing body of the village is a revolutionary committee of twenty-one members—one member from the People's Liberation Army, six cadres, and fourteen members from the mass. We talked at length with members of the revolutionary committee of a particular lane which has a population of 8,000. They told us that their lane is further subdivided into fifty-two groups. A group usually consists of the inhabitants of a building; each group elects a leader and deputy leader, generally retired workers who are not paid for their services. The group leaders organize the retired workers and housewives into groups for the study of Mao Tse-tung thought, arrange for the social services for their neighborhood, mediate quarrels, organize retired workers to provide education for children about the "bitter past" and to do health work. Again, nearly all the leaders and members of the lane revolutionary committees are women.

We asked the cadre to describe some of the social services which the leaders provide. She said that if a mother and father are working and one of the children gets sick, the group leader will arrange for medical care for the child. Or, if the husband is working outside Shanghai, and the wife gives birth to a baby, the leaders will arrange for her to have help in buying food and other needed goods. When there are quarrels within or between families, the leaders gather everyone together and study how Mao's thought applies to the problem. Everyone participates—aged people, "little Red Guards" (children), and workers. An entire building might participate. "By studying Mao's thought," the cadre continued, "one can know objectively who is right and who is wrong. It is very rare that this does not solve the problem."

It is one thing to commit oneself publicly to equality for women and quite another to organize society to make this possible. In addition to establishing nursing rooms, nurseries, and kindergartens, the Chinese have developed an integrated way of living of which Chao Yang is an example. This is enormously helpful to the woman who wishes to have a productive work life and to participate actively in her home life.

A commune, of course, is the prototype of the planned, self-contained community where you eat what you raise, make what you need, live near the people with whom you work, and create a system of interdependence in which nearly all of one's needs are met within the commune. The Shuang Chiao (Double Bridge) People's Commune, twenty miles outside Peking, was established in 1958 and has a population of 38,000. It pro-

Member of the revolutionary committee of the Sing Sing Production Brigade, Shanghai

duces wheat, rice, vegetables, and fruit for consumption within the commune and to feed the people in Peking. The peasants raise cows, horses, pigs (6,000 in 1970), and their specialty—40,000 forced-fed Peking ducks a year. Fishing, forestry, and light industry are also part of the work of the commune. To meet the day-care needs of working mothers and the educational needs of the children, there are nurseries, kindergartens, seven primary schools, and six middle schools. And to meet medical needs, there is a commune hospital and health centers at the brigade and team levels, the intermediate and smallest unit of organization.

Many factories and institutes have built apartments near the working quarters to house the workers. The Third Textile Mill of Peking, for example, 70 percent of whose workers are women, has living quarters, near the factory, for over two thousand families, and has nurseries, primary and middle schools, and barbershops. A dining hall, which we visited, seats two to three thousand people. For twelve to thirteen yuan a month, a fifth of the average factory worker's monthly salary, one can get three meals a day, and we were told that most workers eat most of their meals there.

A brief word on the relative cost of living in China. The average factory worker, we were told, earns about sixty yuan per month. (One yuan is equivalent to forty American cents.) Rent averages less than 5 percent, including utilities; food prepared privately costs slightly more than 25 percent of one's monthly salary, rice and vegetables being the most inexpensive items. Clothes are relatively inexpensive—a man's shirt cost six yuan; a woman's pants and blouse, fourteen yuan; a pair of typical Chinese cloth shoes, 3.70 yuan. Among consumer goods, a bicycle is the first item saved for; and it costs 140 yuan. An alarm clock costs fifteen yuan, and a thermos, seven yuan. The cost of living is set at a low enough level that most families have money left over to save or spend on consumer goods. Life on the communes is, clearly, harder. Income on the communes is apportioned annually or semi-annually according to the number of work points accrued by each individual. (The work-point system is supposedly no longer discriminatory against women. There is, however, great variation with regard to this throughout China and there is evidence that women generally earn less than men.) The range of income in the communes we visited was, we were told, 600 to 1,000 yuan per family per year. Rent is free, as are some of the foods grown in the commune; prices in the commune shops are the same as in city shops.

The Institute for Biological Products in Peking is another self-contained neighborhood including laboratories for scientific work, dormitories for single workers, quarters for married workers, dining halls, a nursery and a primary school, animals for the scientific experiments, plants to feed the animals, and many kinds of people living together who are needed to service the institute—gardeners, grandparents, teachers, medical personnel, scientists, and mechanics. It is a true neighborhood, with large trees, paths leading from the work area to the living quarters and to the nursery, all within easy walking distance. A married worker with children can go to the dining hall for breakfast, drop her child at the nursery, walk to work, return to the dining hall for lunch, work the rest of the day, pick up the child at the nursery, and then either eat with her family in the dining hall or make dinner for them at home.

The "responsible member" of the revolutionary committee at this institute in many ways represents the new role of women in China. She is a plump (just about the only plump person we saw!), laughing woman, a member of the People's Liberation Army, a physician, the wife of a P.L.A. man, the mother of four grown children, and a key administrator at the institute. Assigned by the P.L.A. during the Cultural Revolution, she has been at the institute for three years to aid in its administration. However, she was the only female P.L.A. member we saw assigned to a revolutionary committee; hers is the role the Chinese want to see women play but in actuality they play quite infrequently.

Responsible member of the revolutionary committee, Institute for Biological Products

Self-contained communities are an aid to women who combine home life with productive labor; they can also be of immense help in meeting the needs of all community members. Children have the opportunity to be with people of different ages and occupations; men are close to work and close to home, thereby increasing their activity in both; and the elderly have built-in neighbors and some sort of role that is useful to the society.

We were invited to see some of the apartments at Chao Yang. The first we visited was occupied by a sixty-six-year-old woman, small, bent over, with deep lines on her face. She greeted us happily, perhaps pleased to have foreign guests, perhaps feeling honored that her home was chosen for us to see. She lived alone in one room furnished with a bed and bureau, a table, and two chairs. A lightbulb hung over the table, and the bureau held a radio and some snapshots of small children. A picture of Mao was on the wall. The room was simple but comfortable. She shared a kitchen and bathroom.

She clasped us by the hand, pressed us to sit down, and began to tell us of the "bitter past." Of her seven children, six had died before Liberation because of lack of medical care. Before Liberation she had had no bed and slept on the floor; she had none of the things she had now, she said, waving to include the furnishings. She is retired; she used to work in the textile factory but retired at the age of fifty and receives 70 percent of her salary, or thirty yuan a month. Her rent is three yuan a month, and her food, sixteen to twenty yuan. Her medical care is free; it is paid by the factory. She even puts some of her money aside in a savings account.

Since retirement, she does house cleaning and cooking and talks about the "bitter years" to the local primary-school children so they will understand what life was like before the revolution. We, thinking of the elderly in our country, who are so isolated, asked her if she had friends. She smiled and said, "All my neighbors are my friends."

The attitude of husbands has had to change markedly in the past twenty years for women to be in any sense liberated. We were told frequently that husbands help with the housework, with child-rearing, and with the cooking. Women do more housework than men, however, even though the men help. We wondered whether women perhaps do a full day's work away from the home during the day and then a full day's work at home in the evening. Yet Chinese women do not seem

Elderly woman, Peking

to see the liberation of women in terms of a conflict between men and women. They see the conflict in their society rather as one between new ideas and remnants of feudal thinking.

Premier Chou En-lai, talking with a group of Westerners recently about the equality of women, is reported to have said: ". . . There are still a lot of old customs hindering progress. We must admit the hindrances and support the women—not throw cold water on them. Old customs take effort to overcome. Chairman Mao says, 'Don't believe everything they say if you didn't look into it yourself.' In some places it is just like the old days. First there is a girl born, then a second, third, fourth, until there are nine girls. By that time the wife is forty-five, and only then can she stop trying for a son. Is this equality?" [4]

[4] Audrey Topping: "Return to Changing China," *National Geographic,* December 1971, p. 833.

Premier Chou's comments point up the differences in the role of women in the cities and in the countryside. We were told repeatedly that ideas change more slowly in the rural areas, that parents there still prefer male offspring and have more children. In our travels, we did not find the power of women as pervasive in the communes as in the cities. In general, male representatives from the revolutionary committees greeted us at the communes, whereas female representatives greeted us in the cities. This is quite important, since 80 percent of the people live in the countryside.

But dramatic changes have taken place. And these changes could not have come about had it not been for the help of the husbands and the support of society in general. Liu Jian is a small, vibrant thirty-six-year-old physician who is the head of the health center of the Shuang Chiao People's Commune on the outskirts of Peking. As she showed us around the commune, she told us about her professional career. In 1951 Dr. Liu was a health worker; in 1955 she went on to nursing school for two and a half years. After serving as a nurse in a hospital for three years, she was sent to medical school for two more years. She attended full-time, receiving a half salary, and then returned to the hospital in Peking where she had served. Then two years ago, responding to Mao's call for medical personnel to work in the countryside, she came to this commune to work. Dr. Liu is married and has two sons, eleven and nine. She lives in the commune during the week and goes home to her family on the weekends. I asked how the boys were taken care of while she is away and she replied that they have been in nursery school and kindergarten and "know how to take care of themselves. They eat in the dining halls and their father helps to care for them." At first, she told us, she worried about the children because she and they were not used to living apart, but they have become used to it and are managing now. "One's private life is a small matter; it's the state, the society that is important," she went on to tell us with great feeling. Clearly, she felt her place was here at the commune rather than in Peking with her family, and because of the structure of the society and the support she had at home, she was able to carry on with both.

Chen Hui-cheng is mother, wife, and full-time member of the staff of the Chinese Medical Association. She has three children—two boys, thirteen and eight, and a girl of three. Her oldest child is in junior middle school and the eight-year-old is in primary school; they eat in the dining halls near their home and are in school six days a week. The youngest child lives in a full-time kindergarten for which Comrade Chen pays twelve yuan a month. When Comrade Chen is free on Sundays, she brings her little girl home for the day. I asked how well the child was likely to adjust to living at home when she started primary school at the age of seven, and she assured me that children adjust happily after a brief period of homesickness for the kindergarten. "Chinese women need kindergartens to work for the socialist revolution!" Comrade Chen said with feeling. Comrade Chen, a petite, lively woman in her thirties, was part of the delegation that met my husband and me in Canton and stayed with us during our three-day visit. The group from the Canton Medical Association stayed at the same hotel we did and were "on duty" day and night in case we should need anything.

Dr. Chiang Ray-ling, a tall, slim, soft-spoken thirty-seven-year-old internist at the Friendship Hospital in

Peking, spent one year as a member of the mobile medical team in the countryside in Shensi Province. "After the Cultural Revolution, it became clear that conditions in the countryside were more backward than in the city; the countryside needed more experienced medical care to serve the peasants," Dr. Chiang told us when we visited her hospital. Her mobile medical team was part of the hospital's effort to provide additional resources for rural medical care. Medical personnel go into the countryside, too, to become more familiar with the life of the peasants, to become "reeducated." In the countryside Dr. Chiang lived with the peasants, ate, labored, and collected herb medicines with them. "I witnessed how energetic and how revolutionary their ideology is, what a heroic spirit they have. My sentiments changed and I started to look upon them as members of my own family." Dr. Chiang was in the countryside from May 1970 until July 1971 without once returning to Peking to see her husband and two children, ages eight and two. When I asked her why she had not visited them, she replied, "There was too much work to do." We asked how she found her children when she came home and she said she'd found them grownup "mentally, physically, and culturally. My elder child was elected a leader of his class and joined the Young Pioneers. When he was asked where his mother was, he would answer, 'My mother went to the countryside to serve the poor and lower middle peasants.' I think he was proud of me."

These stories are of course not typical of most women in China today. But the very fact that these women have a higher education, are professionals who can leave their family to work in their professional capacity to help the society is evidence of the enormous strides women have made in China.

In our visits to scientific institutes, hospitals, medical schools, and other professionally staffed institutions, we found that fewer than 50 percent of the professional workers were women, and far fewer women than that were represented in the leading bodies of those institutions. At the Institute of Materia Medica in Peking, for instance, we were told that 40 percent of the workers—both technicians and professionals—were women, but in the group that greeted us (groups that greet foreigners are usually representative of the leading body of an institution) there were seven men and one woman. At the Peking Medical College we were greeted by nineteen persons, five of them women. In the five classes we visited at the medical school there were two women teachers and three men teachers. Women are entering the professions, but they do not seem to hold leadership positions in great numbers. No doubt, the lag must be due to some extent to the relatively recent training of women professionals. In ten or twenty years, when another generation of women has had the opportunity to obtain a higher education, we can look for more women in the revolutionary committees and in other leadership roles.

What of the role of Chinese women as sex objects? How does the society deal with this difficult and subtle problem which exists for all women as well as for all societies? The Chinese have eliminated most forms of outward sexual differentiation. Although there have been variations over the years, currently women's clothing is purely functional, designed to cover and protect, not to delineate or arouse. Women wear baggy pants, generally either navy blue or gray, a white blouse, and a simple button-up-the-front jacket—all loose-fitting. Recent Western visitors report seeing women occasionally in skirts; we only saw teenage girls in skirts on National

Day. Hair is usually cut short, to just below the ear, except for young girls, who wear their hair short or in long pigtails, and their faces are scrubbed clean, without any makeup whatever. It was fascinating to learn from Han Suyin's writings, after we returned home, that Chinese women before Liberation wore long blue dresses, like a uniform, and rarely, if ever, wore makeup. Women wear no jewelry, and that includes wedding rings, but everyone wears a Mao button. Women are addressed as "comrade," not Miss or Mrs., and generally retain their maiden name. There is, of course, no advertising except for the thoughts of Mao, and therefore no sex on billboards. Since the arts deal only with revolutionary themes, never love or sex, women are portrayed in their relationship to their country and more specifically to the revolution.

"The White-Haired Girl," a revolutionary ballet which we saw in Shanghai, tells the story of the daughter of a tenant farmer who cannot meet his payments to the landlord, so the landlord claims the daughter instead. The father tries to intervene and is killed. The girl is taken to the landlord's home and cruelly treated but manages to escape. For years she lives in the hills, barely able to survive; during this period, her hair turns white.

Meanwhile, her boyfriend from their village has joined the Eighth Route Army; he and his comrades find the girl and together they liberate the village, turn over the land to the peasants, and the red sun rises in the east. As they dance off, the implication is, clearly, that they will all, soldiers and peasants, continue the revolution; the message one is left with is not personal but political.

Because of the way women dress and the roles they

A girls' band on National Day

Women performing on National Day

play in society, one tends to see them as persons rather than primarily as women in one's relations with them. With men as well, one finds oneself noticing the shape of the head, the cheekbones, skin color, because clothing provides no clues to individuality. Rather than feeling oppressed by the similarity of Chinese clothing, I soon felt overdressed and began myself not to wear jewelry.

Martin Bernal, comparing life under Communism in China and in North Vietnam, points out the historical and geographical similarities between the two countries but goes on to contrast the women and their outlook on sex. "In China with its unisex clothing, sexual passions run hidden and deep. Vietnamese women in both north and south are beautiful, and they know it. Unlike Chinese women they wear bras even in the country-side. They seem self-conscious and aware of their sexual attractiveness." [5] Bernal does not, however, discuss the place of women in North Vietnamese society or what efforts, if any, have been made to establish equality for women. And we must keep in mind that the Chinese dress alike not only to discourage women from being thought of as sex objects and to foster a sense of equality, but also to discourage materialism and class consciousness.

Returning from China, one questions some basic elements in Western society that are only now starting to be questioned. Is outward sexuality necessary for a healthy and enjoyable sex life? Must sexuality be emphasized in all aspects of life, can't it be a private thing between two people? We can go further and wonder if the Western, particularly the American, emphasis on outward sexuality may not interfere with one's innermost sexual feelings, displacing and obscuring them. We were told by a German physician who has lived in China for thirty years and is now a Chinese citizen that the Chinese attach no sinful feelings to sex, that sex is regarded as a natural function—but a private one. There is, of course, no profit to be made under Chinese Communism by exploiting sex. How much have our sexual attitudes in the West been influenced by commercial exploitation of sexuality? Have we perhaps accepted the advertising man's dream as reality?

[5] Martin Bernal: "North Vietnam and China: Reflections on a Visit," *New York Review of Books,* August 12, 1971, p. 16.

3

Marriage, Pregnancy, and Childbirth

We have continued our work with hygiene and public health all the time, especially since 1958, when we formed the people's commune. The public health work was better organized after that. We go to see the women who are pregnant and talk with them about what to do in their pregnancy. We instruct them in the new delivery art and tell them how to look after their infants . . . We tell the women to let themselves be examined regularly and follow the doctor's advice. We instruct them in birth control and contraceptive methods. The women follow our advice because they have found that with the old methods many children died, but with our new scientific methods both mother and child survive.

LI KUEI-YING,
describing one activity of her party group for women's work, in JAN MYRDAL'S Report from a Chinese Village

LI WEI, A BEAUTIFUL, SLENDER GIRL OF TWENTY-two with two dark pigtails and smiling eyes, is a medical student at the Canton Medical School. After graduation from junior secondary school at the age of eighteen, she joined the People's Liberation Army in 1968. While in the P.L.A., she was assigned to a training class for nurses and worked as a nurse until she was admitted to medical school. After she finishes medical school, she plans to return to her village to practice medicine in the commune in which she was born and raised. She will be twenty-four when she completes her medical training and will not consider marriage until then. Li Wei looks younger than her twenty-two years; by our standards she looks sixteen and has a gay, unsophisticated manner that few American girls have. When we asked her to pose with her fellow medical student Chen Sing-yen, a girl of twenty-two, they put their arms around each other's waist in a warm, comradely way. Because of the lessened emphasis on sex and sexual relationships, people engage in many kinds of warm relationships.

Li Wei will not marry until she is twenty-four, twenty-five, or twenty-six; this is the age at which women are expected to marry. Also, we were told, "students never marry." The ideal marriage age for men, es-

Li Wei and Chen Sing-yen, medical students

tablished by custom (legally, Chinese women can marry at eighteen and men at twenty) is from twenty-six to twenty-nine. A relatively late marriage is advocated for several reasons: it is a form of birth control; too, the Chinese want their young people to spend their early years serving their country and gaining a deeper understanding of its needs. Young people with strong personal attachments would be more reluctant to go into the countryside or to journey to distant lands to help build a canal, say, or offer medical assistance, or help with the planting and harvesting. Late marriage is of course, more prevalent in urban areas, as old ideas linger on in the countryside. Jan Myrdal wrote that, in the early 1960's in Liu Ling Village in northern Shensi Province, girls and boys still married at about twenty.[1] This was prior to the Cultural Revolution, however, and may well have changed.

Divorce is available to everyone. The judge makes an effort to reconcile the couple with the help of friends, family, or the local revolutionary committee, but if reconciliation does not appear feasible, the couple is granted a divorce. However, divorce is relatively rare, we were told: "Why would people want to be divorced when they married of their own volition?" As one notices, the Chinese compare the present wih the past, not with life in other societies.

We were told repeatedly that sexual intercourse is little engaged in before marriage, and Myrdal's report on Liu Ling Village corroborates this. Children born out of wedlock are virtually unheard of, and abortions for unmarried girls are as rare. This lack of premarital sex is surprising to Westerners. But one must remember that, prior to 1949, girls led very restricted lives in China. They married very young and generally, before marriage, had no relationships with men other than members of their family. Women of the middle and upper classes scarcely ventured beyond their own courtyards and, when they did, were accompanied and safeguarded.

In this connection, it is interesting to note the lack of pre-marital sex among Chinese-Americans in the

[1] Jan Myrdal: *Report from a Chinese Village* (New York: New American Library, 1966), p. 54.

United States. We recently talked at length with a number of Chinese-American students, who say that sex before marriage, as well as illegitimacy and abortion, are rare in the Chinese community in this country, but this is slowly changing. One woman medical student felt that Chinese young people simply accept the sexual code handed down from their parents, as they accept Tao, "The Way," or "morality"; these things are not questioned, and one does not decide for oneself, one simply accepts. When I wondered if the men accept these standards too, she said, "Oh, yes. He wouldn't be considered decent if he behaved otherwise." (The students we spoke to felt that theirs was perhaps the last generation to abide by traditional Chinese values. They ascribed the strength of the value system to the closeness of the Chinese family, to the fact that one's identification is primarily with one's family rather than with one's peer group. A law student described growing up with her three younger sisters, within the circle of her family and their family-operated laundry; she linked the closeness of the Chinese family with the prevalence of a family business. This, she felt, made it possible for parents to be home with their children and for children to assume responsibility within the family setting. "My sisters were my friends," she went on. "We did everything together; even when we had other friends, we all moved in the same group."

Another American medical student felt that even when a young person moved out of the Chinese community to go to college, for example, and developed close attachments to non-Chinese friends, the value system engendered by one's family held.

Prostitution was widespread in pre-Liberation China and undoubtedly accounted for much of pre-Liberation sex. Since 1949, prostitution has been eliminated, we were told, as has venereal disease.[2] At Liberation, it has been reported, 10 percent of the population in the national minority areas [3] and 5 percent of the population in the cities and urban areas suffered from syphilis. Following Liberation houses of prostitution were closed and jobs found for the women. They were provided with free medical care and encouraged, through "Speak Bitterness" sessions, to understand the conditions that led them into prostitution. Various methods were used to find and treat people with venereal disease in different parts of the country: in the national minority areas, where there was a high incidence, a survey was made of the entire population; in the cities, steps were taken to find individual cases. Para-professionals were trained, medically and politically, to attack the problem; and health propaganda was widely disseminated on the origin, meaning, symptoms, and treatment of venereal disease. Dr. Ling Chi, a dermatologist in Shanghai, reported that the last case of early syphilis seen in that city occurred in 1958; the last two cases of gonorrhea occurred in 1967; and last case of congenital syphilis, in 1964. Because of the virtual elimination of venereal disease, blood tests before marriage are not used.

During the child-bearing years (which are counted from marriage to menopause), women are urged to practice birth control. Information is widely made

[2] Much of this material on venereal disease is from George Hatem: "With Mao Tse-tung's Thought as the Compass for Action in the Control of Venereal Diseases in China," *China's Medicine,* Volume 1 (October 1966), pp. 52–67.

[3] While the Han people account for over 90 percent of the Chinese people, China still has over 40 million people of different nationalities: Mongols, Tibetans, Kazakhs, Vighurs, and others. There are five national autonomous regions in China.

available with the help of neighborhood health workers, who are recruited from among the women in the neighborhood. Every local street committee and lane committee has its own health center or health station, and the workers are trained to understand birth-control techniques and explain them to the rest of the community. As Chen Hui-cheng told me, two children are considered desirable; some people have three, as she does —but "we are supposed to use birth control to help China." In the countryside, however, families are more apt to have four or five children.

In a lane health center in Peking, we saw a chart listing the five responsibilities of Red Guard doctors who in urban areas serve as counterparts of barefoot doctors. (They study for ten days and then work under the supervision of fully trained doctors.) In fourth place on the chart is family planning. The Red Guard doctor has the responsibility to educate the people regarding family planning. The emphasis on "planned birth"— the Chinese phrase—shows impressive results. The district general hospital, the parent body of the neighborhood health clinic, reported that, of all the families living in their district, which has a population of 49,-300, 84 percent use some method of birth control. The most popular were oral contraceptives, intra-uterine contraceptive devices, and tubal ligations; vasectomies were also being done but were not as popular.

In Hangchow, the Silvery Lane Health Center has organized health workers from every block in the lane. The more populous lanes have seven health workers, and the more sparsely populated lanes as few as two. The health workers are women volunteers who live in the lane in which they work; 80 percent have other jobs, and the rest are retired. They are trained by Red Guard doctors and by doctors from the district hospital; after they begin work they gather occasionally to compare experiences. Each month the health workers go from door to door to determine what method of birth control each woman in the block is using. A chart is kept on the wall of the health center indicating how many women use what kind of contraception (Figure 1, below).

Figure 1

FAMILY PLANNING CHART
SILVERY LANE HEALTH STATION, HANGCHOW

	Number	*Percent*	
Total number of married women	369	100%	
Permanently sterilized	99	27%	
Vasectomies	10		3%
Tubal ligation	89		24%
Total using contraceptives	172	46%	
Oral contraceptives	65		17%
Condom	69		19%
IUCD	22		6%
Rhythm	7		2%
Other	9		2%
Not using contraceptives	88	24%	
Husband outside the city	21		6%
"Has not been pregnant"	6		2%
Breast feeding	16		4%
Newly married	7		2%
Chronically ill	13		3%
Other	25		7%
Abortions	0	0%	
Pregnant	10	3%	
Birth rate (January–September 1971)		5.9/1000	

Several interesting aspects of birth control can be noted from the chart. (1) The diaphragm is not used at all. (2) Rhythm is used very little. (3) When the husband is not living at home but working in another city or in the countryside, there is no need for birth control, which indicates that extramarital sex is minimal. (4) Vasectomies exist, but tubal ligations are nine times more common. (5) No abortions have been performed since January (a period of nine months), and only four abortions were done in 1970. We wondered if some of the women were not reluctant to talk about the birth-control techniques they used. Some of the women were shy, we were told, but after they were reeducated, they didn't mind discussing these things. A newly married woman might hesitate. In that case, the cadre from the block and the health worker visit her to explain the importance of birth control; she soon overcomes her resistance. (Of course, as has been noted by many visitors to China, the Chinese have a different concept of privacy than we in the West do. They never hesitated to tell us their age, for example, or their salary. Perhaps birth-control methods are now thought of in the same way.)

On the communes, the midwives provide birth-control information. Chou Shu-ping, the midwife at the Double North Production Team, which is part of the Double Bridge People's Commune outside Peking, told us that the main methods of birth control used by her production team (pop. 509) were the intra-uterine device, oral contraceptives, tubal ligations, and condoms. The woman makes the choice, with the advice of the midwife and possibly the doctor at the health center. I.U.D.'s are inserted at the health center and tubal ligations are usually done after two or three children have been born. Chou Shu-ping said that some women want tubal ligations and others are persuaded through "propaganda."

In the Health Center of the Mai Chia Wu Production Brigade of the West Lake People's Commune outside Hangchow, the midwife, a twenty-seven-year-old woman, has been trained both as midwife and as barefoot doctor, with six months of training at the commune hospital. Primarily responsible for educating the members of the brigade about birth control, she indicated that condoms and rings were the most popular form of contraception. Clearly, there is some variation in the popularity of various birth-control methods.

Many techniques are being used in China's campaign to lower the birth rate—education, the wide distribution of contraceptives, the employment of local health workers to disseminate information, and public opinion. However, the element that is especially Chinese and that makes the others work is that families have been convinced that limiting the number of children will help China, and helping China is something they want to do. The poster shown on page 56 was hanging in the Mai Chia Wu Brigade Health Center and illustrates this point graphically. The poster is called: "Plan for Good Birth Control for Revolution." It shows a barefoot doctor holding a book entitled "Late Marriage and Plan for Birth Control: Collection of Information and Experience." Her medical bag is inscribed: "Wei Renmin Fuwu"—"Serve the People."

The captions for the pictures around the periphery give the reasons for practicing "planned birth." They are (clockwise, starting at the top right-hand corner): (1) In order to study and apply Chairman Mao's thought in a lively way. (2) In order to consolidate the proletarian dictatorship. (3) In order to prepare against war, prepare against national disaster, and for the people. (4) In order to support world revolution. (The poster the workers are holding reads: "People of the Whole World, Unite to Defeat the American Imperialists and All Their Running Dogs"—Mao Tse-tung.) (5) In order to cultivate successors to the proletarian revolution. (The sign behind the teacher and student reads: "Study Well and Make Progress Every Day.") (6) In order to grasp revolution, promote production, carry on work, and to prepare against war.

Thus, it is not simply that planned birth is good for the individual, though that is pointed out; it is not simply that raising many children is difficult, though that

Birth-control poster in Hangchow commune

is said; it is not even that having many children interferes with the mother's participation in productive labor, though that is included. Planned birth is important to strengthen the political values the people are taught to believe in. And, above all, planned birth is a direct contribution that every young couple can make to the building of China. Limiting one's family becomes a gain for society, not an individual loss, and some of the zeal attached to other revolutionary values such as working to prevent famine or studying Mao's works rubs off on the issue of birth control. Ivan Illich has said that the poor are not going to give up having large numbers of children until they receive a meaningful piece of the political pie—i.e., power. The Chinese have politicized birth control as they do everything else. Above all, they believe in "putting politics in command."

Although we were unable to obtain national statistics on the current Chinese birth rate, we did learn that the birth rate in Shanghai in 1971 was six to seven per thousand per year, and in Silvery Lane in Hangchow it was 5.9 per thousand per year. However, in one commune, we were told the birth rate was eighteen to twenty per thousand. Even if these figures are not typical of the country as a whole, they are remarkably low in comparison with the birth rate of about forty-five births per thousand in China prior to 1949 and the current birth rate of thirty to forty per thousand in countries of economic development comparable to China's. The Chinese statistics must also be compared with those for the United States as a whole—about seventeen births per thousand—and with the rate in urban ghettos of the United States, about twenty-five per thousand.

At the Institute for Materia Medica in Peking we were told by two women scientists who were working on contraception that a twenty-two-day pill is widely used, particularly in Peking and Shanghai. They are concerned about the side effects and are working on lowering the dosage. They have produced a once-a-month pill and are working on a once-in-three-months and a once-a-year pill. The pill they use, they were quick to tell us, is one the Chinese themselves developed.

Chinese scientists have also worked hard to develop a simple method for the early detection of pregnancy for use particularly in the countryside. Scientists at the Institute for Biological Products told us that in 1966–67 they developed a test involving two solutions which can be preserved for six months at room temperature; it can be performed with simple instruments. One drop of each solution is mixed with one drop of the woman's urine; within three minutes the barefoot doctor can determine whether the patient is pregnant or not. If the solution becomes milky, the woman is pregnant; if it is clear, she is not. This test, we were told, is 95 percent accurate, and the cost is one Chinese cent per test.

Contraception is free, and so is abortion. Abortions, available on the request of the woman alone, are encouraged after the birth of two children and are generally performed only during the first three to three and a half months of pregnancy. Edgar Snow has reported watching an abortion performed by suction curettage, with acupuncture anesthesia. In the Friendship Hospital in Peking, abortions are performed in the Outpatient Department by physicians. When the abortion is performed within fifty days of conception, the woman has ten days off from work. When it is done from fifty

to a hundred and twenty days of pregnancy—
something which is not usual—she has a month off
from work. The emphasis, however, is on "planned
birth" and the use of contraceptives rather than abortion.

In rural areas, abortions are usually performed within
three and a half months after conception, and most
often in a commune hospital or health center, by a regular doctor. The suction method is used. In the
Hangchow Tea Brigade Health Center, for example,
abortions are sometimes performed in the brigade
health center rather than at the commune hospital, and
an electric suction machine is used which is brought
from the commune hospital to the brigade health center. We were told repeatedly that no stigma is attached
to abortion but that abortions are rarely performed on
single women.

In the cities, all babies are delivered in hospitals. In
the Silvery Lane Health Center in Hangchow there
were fifteen births in the past year, all in the hospital;
deliveries at home, they claim, have been eliminated.
Pre-natal care in the urban areas begins with the first
examination, at three to six months of pregnancy. After
that, the woman is examined once a month; after seven
months, she is examined every two weeks. Near term,
the frequency of the examination depends on her con-
dition. Thinking of the situation in the United States,
where many mothers—particularly among the poor—
have no pre-natal care, we asked Dr. Hsu, our interpreter, who is the deputy head of the Department of
Internal Medicine at the East Is Red Hospital in
Shanghai, how widespread pre-natal care is in China.
He told us that that was no longer a problem in China,
since the masses have basic knowledge about pre-natal

care. Also, all women who are to give birth in the hospital need to have been examined prior to the time of delivery, so they do have pre-natal care. Contraceptives and abortions are free, but pre-natal care and childbirth are not. The first visit costs twenty Chinese cents, and the second, ten Chinese cents. For an uncomplicated delivery, the hospital stay is from three to five days and there is a slight fee.

A brief word on the cost of medical care. In the urban areas, medical care, both inpatient and outpatient, is free to government and factory workers and half price to their families. Since 90 percent of the women work and in the cities the great majority would work either for the government or in a factory, most adults are covered. Medical care for children is provided free in school, and immunizations are free to everyone. Other medical care for children is available at half the cost. All hospitalized patients pay a small amount for their food, and those who are not covered by free medical care pay a small amount per day. At the Friendship Hospital in Peking, we were told the cost is one yuan per day, but the doctors made it clear that if the patient could not pay, other financial arrangements were made. In the countryside, many communes have instituted a cooperative system of medical care such as the one organized by the Mai Chia Wu Production Brigade outside Hangchow, whereby each member who joins the cooperative pays a yuan a year, including children, and is entitled to free medical care for the year. New members, including newborn babies, can join the cooperative medical system in September or in March. If an infant needs medical attention before his parents have enrolled him, they pay for his care until the next membership date. If a commune member is hospitalized, the cooperative or the brigade pays for the hospitalization.

In the countryside, most children are born at home. Midwives assist at the delivery and call upon the nearby commune hospital for help when necessary. In both the cities and the countryside, no anesthesia is used in uncomplicated deliveries; in difficult deliveries, acupuncture or other anesthesia is used. The training of midwives varies from place to place, since medicine, like so much else in China, is decentralized. At the Double Bridge Commune, the midwife is trained for two or three months; at the Sing Sing Production Brigade, the midwife was trained for three months in the county hospital. In the Hangchow Tea Brigade, the midwife/barefoot doctor was trained for six months in the commune hospital.

Pre-natal care also varies in the countryside. At the Double Bridge Commune, the barefoot doctor visits the expectant mother in her home after the fifth month and examines her at monthly intervals. She tests her blood pressure and her urine routinely and educates her about her pregnancy. In the Hangchow Tea Brigade, the expectant mother is examined monthly after the first two months, deliveries are in the home, and difficult deliveries at the Hangchow Municipal Hospital. In the Sing Sing Production Brigade, the barefoot doctor goes to the expectant mother's home and examines her every month up to the seventh month, twice a month during the eighth month, and weekly during the last month. She examines her blood pressure and urine, checks the fetal heart, the mother's heart, and the position of the fetus.

The mother is entitled to switch to light work in her fifth or eighth month of pregnancy, depending upon where she lives. There is some variation in length of maternity leave; in some communes she has fifty-six days off, as women do in the city, and in others she returns to light work after thirty days and to regular work after four months.

Though there are variations within the system, there are many similarities as well. Pre-natal care seems to be universal, and delivery is without anesthesia, both in the cities and in the countryside. Mothers in the city are entitled to paid maternity leave; in the countryside, maternity leave is not paid, but the woman does not lose seniority, no matter how long she is away from work. In the countryside we were told everywhere that childbirth is at home, attended by a midwife; in the city, that it is in the hospital, with a doctor in charge.

Virtually all mothers breast-feed their babies until they are a year or a year and a half old. Supplementary bottles are used only when necessary, and children are weaned directly from the breast to the cup.

Medical care for infants and small children is dispensed by the same medical personnel who care for adults. If barefoot doctors dispense primary care, they also treat the children; pediatricians exist as specialists in hospitals.

Since infectious disease was in large part responsible for the high mortality rate in China before 1949, immunizations are an important part of the medical care of children in China today. Every place we visited, the medical workers were very proud of the high percentage of children who are being immunized and the sharp drop in the incidence of infectious disease. Figure 2 indicates the diseases against which children are protected, the age at which the initial immunization is given, and the age at which boosters are given. Figure 3

Figure 2

CHILDHOOD IMMUNIZATIONS

Type of Immunization	*Initial*	*Booster*
Tuberculosis (BCG immunization)	Within 3 days of birth	If tuberculin test becomes negative
Triple immunization (Diphtheria, pertusis, tetanus)	3 monthly doses at 3–6 months	Ages 3 and 6
Poliomyelitis (oral)	3 monthly doses at approximately 6 months	Ages 1 and 5–7
Measles	6–8 months (to children with no history of measles)	Every 3–5 years
Smallpox (vaccination)	6 months (if no contraindication such as eczema exists)	Every 6 years
Encephalitis B	12 months	Annually in October or November up to age 14
Meningitis	12 months	Annually in October or November up to age 14

Figure 3

IMMUNIZATION RATES AT A LANE HEALTH
STATION IN PEKING

Immunization	Number Eligible	Number Immunized	Percent Immunized
Measles	160	156	97.5
Poliomyelitis	164	164	100.0
DPT	163	163	100.0
Encephalitis	119	112	94.1
Meningitis	136	132	97.0
B.C.G.	164	163	98.1
Smallpox	163	135	80.9

indicates the percentage of children immunized during 1970 in a lane health station under the direction of the District General Hospital. We were amazed at the high percentage of children who received the first six immunizations, and surprised at the relatively low percentage who received smallpox vaccinations. We asked about this and were told that if there are contraindications such as eczema, the immunization is not given, as the complications from the vaccination are potentially more dangerous than the possibility of smallpox.

Again thinking of the difficulties of providing regular and adequate medical care to children in our urban ghettos and some of our rural areas, we asked how they managed to immunize such a high percentage of children. We were told that a card is kept on each child and when it is time for immunization or a booster, the mother is notified by a Red Guard doctor and brings the child to the neighborhood health center or the hospital. Occasionally, if the mother is too busy to bring the child, the doctor will go to the home. Clearly, the

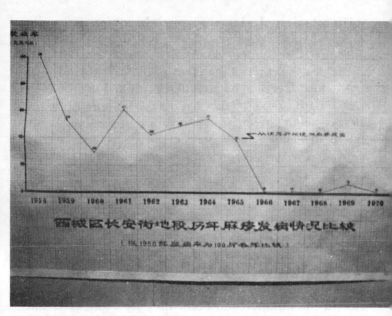

Incidence of measles, 1958–1970

high degree of cooperation on the part of the mothers is due to a large extent to the amount of health education that is carried out with specific reference to infectious diseases. (Mass meetings and smaller study groups are regularly held to teach people how to prevent infectious disease.) Also, the highly organized block system which the Chinese have evolved assures that every family is known to someone connected with the health center.

The use of oral polio immunization began in 1959–60, with a subsequent decrease in reported cases of polio in the district. Polio, like measles, the incidence of which is shown in the chart above, has almost disappeared. Measles immunization began in 1965.

Diphtheria and whooping cough have also almost disappeared. Families have been instructed, when an infectious disease does occur, to report it immediately to the health center. Treatment is given in the hospital or the health center by a regularly trained doctor. The Red Guard doctor makes a home visit, questions the mother about the onset of the illness and whether others in the family have been exposed, isolates the patient, and treats other members of the family if necessary.

Young children are cared for medically in the neighborhood health center and also in the nursery or kindergarten. The kindergarten of the Peking No. 3 Cotton Mill has a pediatrician, Dr. Niu Jen-sheng, who makes rounds every day. According to Dr. Niu, "the only infectious diseases we had in the past year were a few light cases of chicken pox and mumps. We put the kids in the isolation ward and they soon got well. The children are all innoculated against polio, encephalitis, measles, and tuberculosis."

Yung Ping, who works in a nursery in Shanghai, told us that in her nursery, which has 150 children from ages one and a half to three and a half, a doctor looks at the children every morning to check on their physical well-being and also on their "spirits." The doctor checks to see if they are "taking their food properly, how they feel, if they are in high spirits." If they are in low spirits, she tries to determine why—is the child ill, has the child quarreled, has the child just returned from a visit home and is homesick? The first goal of her nursery, Comrade Yung said, is to "keep the children fit and strong physically, for they will be the workers of the future; they will have to be healthy enough to participate in the planting and in the harvesting." The chil-

dren undergo a physical examination before being admitted to the nursery and yearly after admission. Both
at home and at school, great attention is paid to the
physical well-being of the small child.

4

The Cultural Revolution
and the Organization
of Child Care

*Before the Cultural Revolution the children
used to be taught to co-exist with the bourgeoisie
and to be the successors of the bourgeoisie. But
now we believe that education should be revo-
lutionized and must serve the proletariat.*

COMRADE GAO
*teacher in the Yu Yao Road
Kindergarten, Shanghai*

"THEY USED TO DANCE LIKE SWANS AND PLAY like kings and queens; it used to be forbidden for them to have military training and to tell revolutionary stories," we were told by the responsible member of the revolutionary committee of the Pai Hai Kindergarten in Peking. "We have realized since the Cultural Revolution that the education of children is important to the success of the party and to the consolidation of the proletarian dictatorship."

We sat around the conference table, Vic and I, Dr. Hsu, Mr. Hsu, and other physicians who accompanied us, drinking green tea out of mugs with detachable covers, which keep the tea warm, and occasionally glanced at pictures of Marx, Engels, Lenin, and Stalin on one wall, and a larger picture of Mao on the opposite wall. The slight, forty-year-old teacher went on to tell us that their "class consciousness has been raised" since the Cultural Revolution. "Education should serve the workers. Our goal is to train children by means of socialist education and socialist culture to be the successors to the socialist cause."

To understand something of the change that has taken place in the goals and methodology of child care in China today it is necessary to go back and look, even if just briefly, at some of the vicissitudes that educational policy in China has undergone since 1949. After Liberation, the Chinese leadership faced two central problems in the sphere of education: the need to train specialists, such as physicians, scientists, and engineers, and the desire to create a classless society in which no elite would exist, whether based on power or on education. A basic conflict exists between these two goals, and much of Chinese educational policy has derived from the effort to deal with this conflict.

The Chinese were also faced with the traditional divorce between physical and intellectual labor which Isaac Deutscher characterizes as the "divorce that has been at the root of man's estrangement from man, of mankind's division into rulers and ruled and into antagonistic classes . . ." [1]

The chasm between manual and intellectual labor had been particularly wide in pre-Liberation China, where the mandarin scholars, with their long robes and long fingernails, felt "profound contempt and revulsion" toward manual labor.[2] It has been a central goal of the Chinese Communists to bridge this chasm, to integrate physical labor into the education process, thereby eliminating or reducing the traditional disdain for peasants and workers. This dilemma, far older than the Chinese revolution, is one which other societies, including Israel and the Soviet Union, have tried with great difficulty to deal with.

In the early to mid-1950's, much of Chinese higher education was remodeled on a Soviet pattern. "In the classroom, emphasis was placed on scientific professionalism and technical expertise. Marxist political re-edu-

[1] Isaac Deutscher: "On Socialist Man" (New York: Merit Publications, 1967), p. 10.
[2] Han Suyin: "Reflections on Social Change," *Bulletin of the Atomic Scientists,* Vol. 22, No. 6 (June 1966), p. 82.

cation and manual labor were relegated to a secondary position despite the efforts of many Party Cadres to stress them." [3] Because the emphasis was on training technicians as rapidly as possible, the universities tended to admit the best-qualified students; this meant that student enrollment was biased in favor of students from bourgeois families. In 1958, over 70 percent of the students came from bourgeois families.[4] Another elite was being built upon the elite which had existed prior to Liberation.

In a country in which the overwhelming majority consists of poor, uneducated, or slightly educated peasants, the potential power of a technical elite is enormous. It was necessary, therefore, to democratize enrollment in higher education and to spread scientific knowledge as widely as possible among the people. In June 1957, Mao initiated the "Great Leap Forward," which encompassed educational revolution as an integral part. Admissions policies were changed to admit more workers and peasants. Politics was stressed and manual labor was combined with academic work. At Peking University, for example, students helped to build the Ming Tung Reservoir. The new educational policies can perhaps be best described by quoting the president of Tsinghua University: "The educational institution becomes not just a school, but at the same time a research institute, factory, designing institute, and building concern. An end is put to the traditional concept of a school as a consumer unit, an ivory tower (far removed) from social life. Our policy bridges the gap between educational and production units." [5]

---

[3] Victor Nee: *The Cultural Revolution at Peking University* (New York: Monthly Review Press, 1969), p. 13.
[4] Ibid., p. 13.
[5] Ibid., pp. 21–22.

But conflict continued between raising the educational and intellectual standards and "putting politics in command," otherwise known as being "red and expert." In the early 1960's, officials at Peking University, wanting to uphold its honor among academic institutions and undoubtedly feeling that producing highly trained specialists was the way to China's advancement, instituted a formal academic hierarchy based solely on academic standards. Academic achievement was stressed to students as well as teachers, and as competition increased, political activity declined. With greater competition, students recruited from the countryside who had received schooling inferior to that of students from the city began to feel inadequate. They could not compete academically; moreover, ideology and political work, at which they excelled, was being deemphasized.

The explosive educational situation in the mid-1960's was exacerbated by the differentiation between primary and secondary schools. After Liberation, an enormous school-construction program was launched in which most schools were designed to include "half work and half study." These schools were primarily in the countryside. In the cities, most of the schools were academic full-time and prepared students much more adequately for the university. In addition to these discrepancies, boarding schools existed for the children of cadres. These were a leftover from the 1930's and 1940's, when cadres, fighting with the Eighth Route Army or organizing villages in the liberated areas, could not care for their own children. During this period, there was an egalitarian, revolutionary flavor to these boarding schools. After Liberation, however, the schools became yet another privilege enjoyed by the cadres, who were beginning to constitute a privileged class. To make matters worse, in May 1963 a system of elite schools was established. Out of a group of selected primary and secondary schools, 36 secondary schools and 162 primary schools were selected and resources and manpower concentrated there.[6] By 1965, China in fact had separate facilities to train intellectual workers and others to train physical laborers. A hierarchy had been set up which was likely to perpetuate a class society based on education and power to replace the earlier class distinctions based on money and land.

These were some of the factors that, along with a number of political issues, led Nieh Yuan-tsu and six other philosophy instructors at Peking University to put up the first "big-character poster," (a newspaper written in large characters which was put up on a wall) on May 25, 1966, just after two in the afternoon. And so the Great Proletarian Cultural Revolution was launched. Mao was out of Peking during this time, but when he returned, he put up his own "big-character poster," which gave clear support to the rebels. The Cultural Revolution was a time of profound reexamination of the direction in which all segments of the society were moving, a reexamination of the role of the Communist Party, of the role of the cadres, and a reassessment of the techniques for running institutions within the society. It was a rebellion against elitism, professionalism, and credentialism for their own sake. More specifically, the Cultural Revolution reaffirmed Mao's principle of "putting politics in command"; being "red" took precedence over being "expert." The Cultural Revolution disavowed the use of economic incentives as a road to capitalism and substituted "spiri-

[6] Ibid., p. 38.

tual and moral incentives," working for the good of all instead of for oneself.[7] The "mobilization of the mass" became the way to economic reconstruction, rather than specialization and bureaucratism—which has come to be known in China as the Russian way. Mao's belief in the malleability of man, the perfectability of man through an educational system encompassing not only traditional schooling but also the inculcation of socialist values, emerged from that hectic period as the prevailing ideology. Much of this ideology has roots in past Chinese philosophy—Mencius' view of the essential goodness of man, Wang Fu-chih's belief in the malleability of man, and the Confucian stress on education.[8]

The Cultural Revolution asserted, as well, the invincibility of Mao's ideology and repudiated the ideas of those who opposed him, as exemplified by Liu Shao-ch'i, the former Chairman of the People's National Congress and constitutional chief of state, who was condemned for following "the capitalist road." For many young Chinese, "the Cultural Revolution represented a personal recommitment to revolutionary values." [9]

The Cultural Revolution was not over even in September–October of 1971, when we were in China. Peking University did not reopen until the fall of 1970; many of the institutions that we visited were still undergoing "struggle, criticism, and transformation"; medical schools were just starting classes again; and schools for kindergarten teachers had not been started

[7] Jerome Ch'en, ed., *Mao* (Englewood Cliffs, N.J.: Prentice-Hall, Inc., 1969), pp. 35–37.

[8] Ibid., p. 33.

[9] B. Michael Frolic: "What the Cultural Revolution Was All About," *The New York Times Magazine*, October 24, 1971, p. 115.

up at all. Many institutions had not reopened because the leading bodies of those institutions had not yet decided what educational direction to take.

The main task of kindergarten teachers before the Cultural Revolution was to provide "food, clothing, and shelter" for the children, but, according to Comrade Gao, a teacher in the Yu Yao Road Kindergarten, Shanghai, they "gave no thought to ideological education." They gave children only "education of a mother's love," but this education was "without any class feeling or class sympathy." This description of the goals of child care prior to the Cultural Revolution is not borne out, however, by reports from China in the 1950's and early 1960's. Felix Greene, in his visit to the Pai Hai Kindergarten in 1960, was told by the head teacher: " 'Our children . . . when they grow up, will take their place in the country's work—they will be children trained in communist ideals. They will love labor. They will respect people . . . These principles are taught according to age levels, in conversation, songs, nursery rhymes, art and games!' " [10] There is also a study done by a Canadian child psychiatrist in 1961 to determine some of the attitudes of young people, ages ten to sixteen, and the character traits "which the Chinese leaders have been trying to form in these youth over the last 12 years . . ." The most frequent answers to the question "What is the most favorable thing that someone could say about you?" were: "She does her best for the mother-country." "He is a good student and a good worker." "He is selflessly devoted to the cause." The most common answers to the question "What is the best act you could perform?" were: "Help an old

[10] Felix Greene: *China* (New York: Ballantine Books, 1962), p. 50.

person carry his packages." "Help reconcile children who are fighting." "Contribute to the success of the Agricultural Plan by growing a garden." [11] Obviously, the Chinese were "giving thought to ideological education" before the Cultural Revolution, and much of the deprecating of the goals and methods of education prior to 1966 is an exaggeration. It is likely that the changes with respect to pre-school education since the Cultural Revolution are ones of degree rather than basic changes in philosophy.

Before the Cultural Revolution, children attended primary school for six years, junior middle school for three years, and a select few attended senior middle school for three years. Much variation exists now, but generally children attend primary school for five years and junior middle school for three years. Prior to 1966, graduation from senior middle school was required for admission to the university, medical school, or teachers' school; at present a student needs only to have finished junior middle school, after which he must work for two to three years in a commune or a factory, or possibly in the People's Liberation Army, and then perhaps go on for more education.

The teacher-training program consisted of the following sequences. During the first year, teachers had the same basic courses as they would have had in senior middle school: math, physics, chemistry, biology, history, Chinese literature, one foreign language—English or Russian—and, in addition, piano, drawing, music, and gym. In the second year, they attended education courses, courses in child psychology, and courses in

[11] Denis Lazure: "The Family and Youth in New China: Psychiatric Observations," *Canadian Medical Association Journal*, Vol. 86 (January 27, 1962), pp. 179–83.

child health. The third year continued some of the previous courses as well as observation and practice teaching in a local nursery every week or every two weeks during the second half of the year. With this curriculum in mind, it is easy to understand the questioning of the need for physics, chemistry, and biology in the training of kindergarten teachers. As there have been no graduates since 1966 (the onset of the Cultural Revolution), I wondered where new teachers were coming from and was told that people were learning teaching on-the-job.

In any case, up to the time of our visit, the Chinese had not yet decided what kind of training was appropriate for kindergarten teachers. Since the Cultural Revolution, the goals of nursery and kindergarten teaching too have undergone "struggle, criticism, and transformation." It has been decided, as Joan Robinson phrases it, that "proletarian socialism requires acquisitiveness to be replaced by a spirit of service." [12] What has not been determined is what form of teacher training will most actively promote this spirit.

Within the broad general goal of "training the children to become workers with a socialist consciousness and with socialist culture," many other goals exist. To understand these, let us look briefly at some of the writings of Mao Tse-tung, which have communicated a system of values to the great mass of the people.

Mao's writings fill many volumes and range in time from the 1920's to the 1960's. Since the Cultural Revolution, his writings have been elevated, essentially, to an infallible body of thought that is constantly referred to. They are the principal vehicle for bringing an en-

[12] Joan Robinson: *The Cultural Revolution in China* (Baltimore, Maryland: Penguin Books, 1969), p. 12.

tire population from a feudal way of thinking characterized, by superstition, fatalism, and illiteracy to a modern, scientific outlook. The Chinese have attempted to bridge this enormous gap in one generation. As Han Suyin has written, "the eradication of the feudal mind is not an easy process . . . It means getting the masses away from the anchored belief that natural calamities are 'fixed by heaven' and that therefore nothing can be done to remedy one's lot . . ." [13] Not only did floods, typhoons, and illness have to be explained, but people had to be convinced that they could overcome such calamities. In addition, a new morality had to be taught, one based on the new economic and political goals of post-Liberation China.

The writings of Mao most frequently referred to are the "Three Constantly Read Articles" (in the order in which they appear and in which they are always spoken of): "Serve the People," written in 1944; "In Memory of Norman Bethune," written in 1939; and "The Foolish Old Man Who Removed the Mountains," written in 1945. These articles so pervade the thinking of the Chinese people today, especially since the Cultural Revolution, that it is truly impossible to understand Chinese society without understanding them.

"Serve the People" was written during the Sino-Japanese War when the Communist Party and the Eighth Route Army were struggling against both the Japanese and the Kuomintang. In this brief essay, Mao exhorts the soldiers: "The Chinese people are suffering; it is our duty to save them and we must exert ourselves in struggle. Wherever there is struggle there is sacrifice, and death is a common occurrence." He tells them that

[13] Suyin, "Reflections on Social Change," p. 81.

dying for the "interest of the people" is a "worthy death" but reminds them to "avoid unnecessary sacrifices." "Our cadres must show concern for every soldier and all people in the revolutionary ranks must care for each other, must love and help each other." This, then, is the message of the first article—that one's task is to "serve the people" and to "care for each other, love and help each other." [14]

In the second essay, "In Memory of Norman Bethune," Mao tells about the famous thoracic surgeon from Canada who in 1938 went to China to work with the Eighth Route Army in their "war of resistance against Japan." He ministered to the people and soldiers in the Wutai Mountains and died in 1939 of septicemia. Mao eulogizes Bethune, pointing out that he was an example of internationalism in which the proletariat of capitalist countries supports the struggle for liberation of colonial and semi-colonial peoples. Bethune's internationalism and his selflessness, shown in his "boundless sense of responsibility in his work and his boundless warm heartedness toward all comrades and the people," make him a national hero in China today, a model for all the people. [15]

"The Foolish Old Man Who Removed the Mountains" is a parable. Let me quote from Mao: "It tells of an old man who lived in northern China long, long ago and was known as the Foolish Old Man of North Mountain. His house faced South and beyond his doorway stood the two great peaks, Taihang and Wangwu, obstructing the way. With great determination, he led his sons in digging up these mountains hoe in hand.

[14] Mao Tse-tung: *Five Articles* (Peking: Foreign Language Press, 1968), pp. 3–4.
[15] Ibid., p. 7.

Another greybeard, known as the Wise Old Man, saw them and said derisively, 'How silly of you to do this! It is quite impossible for you few to dig up those two huge mountains.' The Foolish Old Man replied, 'When I die, my sons will carry on; when they die, there will be my grandsons, and then their sons and grandsons, and so to infinity. High as they are, the mountains cannot grow any higher and with every bit we dig, they will be that much lower!' [16] And this is the message of the third "Constantly Read Article," that if one mobilizes the people, and their sons and their grandsons, there is nothing one cannot accomplish.

Above all, the children are taught "Wei renmin fuwu"—"Serve the people." They are taught to "care for each other, love and help each other." They are trained to love Chairman Mao and to love their country. They are trained to love the workers, peasants, and soldiers, and to love physical labor. They are taught to "keep only the public good in mind."

Since the Cultural Revolution, with its revolt against elitism and against the Soviet brand of socialism, which the Chinese feel has been distorted by strong elements of consumerism, the Chinese are attempting to fashion a human being who will put the needs of the society before his own, who will identify with those in the society who do the menial labor, who will integrate intellectual labor and physical labor, and who will be motivated by altruism rather than by self-interest. They start with the child in the nursing room and, using a variety of techniques and skills, attempt by the time he is seven years old to inculcate him with these values. The training, of course, does not stop at this point, for

[16] Ibid., pp. 13–14.

the Chinese would be the first to say that people need "education and reeducation," and indeed we had the feeling that education to live in their environment never ceases.

Fifty-six days after the birth of a baby, the Chinese mother usually returns to her work. From this time until the child enters primary school at age seven, the mother has several choices of child care: to be one of the 10 percent who do not work and take care of her child herself; to let her baby be taken care of by a grandparent; to work out an arrangement with a friend or neighbor; or to use the public child-care facilities which have been provided, such as the nursing room, the nursery, and the kindergarten.

With an infant, the most usual thing is for the mother to take him to work with her and leave him in a nursing room. Since most mothers breast-feed their babies, this is by far the most convenient arrangement. The mother is allowed to leave her work and feed her baby twice during the day. Children generally are cared for in the nursing room until they are a year and a half and have been weaned.

When the child is a year and a half, the parents either bring him to a nursery or leave him at home with grandparents. The percentage of children who attend nurseries varies from institution to institution, city to city, and most dramatically from city to countryside. Most often, we were told that 50 percent of city children from the ages of one to roughly three attend nurseries; the other 50 percent remain at home, mostly with grandparents. These percentages are lower in the countryside, where fewer children go to nurseries.

The figures for kindergarten show a much greater number attending than staying home. The children attend kindergarten from age three until they enter primary school at seven; while over 80 percent of the children in urban areas attend kindergarten, this number is clearly lower in the rural areas. Whereas nurseries in general are located at the site of employment, kindergartens are located in the neighborhoods where people live, probably for two reasons: (1) When the child is younger, the parents may feel that they should be closer to him and therefore bring him to a nursery where one of them works. (2) Kindergartens, being more elaborate enterprises, require more space and are therefore housed more often in a separate building rather than in a section of a factory or a hospital or a scientific institution.

Child care in the communes seems more casual, more relaxed, than child care in the cities. Since fewer children attend, units such as the nursing room and the nursery, or the nursery and the kindergarten, are often combined. These facilities are organized both at the production-team (the smallest unit) and the production-brigade (the intermediate) level, not at the commune level. For example, in the Sing Sing Production Brigade, the nursery takes children from fifty-six days to four years of age. However, there is no kindergarten in this production brigade; the grandparents take care of children from four to seven years old, or the mothers care for each other's children. In the Double Bridge Commune, we were told by a representative of the revolutionary committee, each production team has its own nursery and kindergarten. The nursery generally takes children from one month to two years of age and the kindergarten from age two to six. In this commune, however, most of the children remain in their own family units and are taken care of by grandparents until they go to primary school.

Another pattern of child care in the commune is for mothers to place their children in the nursery or kindergarten during the harvest or during other busy seasons when the women are needed to work in the fields. According to Li Kuei-ying of Liu Ling, the village Myrdal studied, "during harvest and ploughing, the women who are pregnant and the old ones with small, crippled feet do the work in the day nursery and the collective dining hall. All the others are out in the fields." [17]

Kindergartens in the neighborhoods are run by revolutionary committees consisting, as do other revolutionary committees, of members of the People's Liberation Army, cadres, and representatives from the "mass." In some revolutionary committees, the P.L.A. has been replaced by members of Mao Tse-tung thought groups who are workers at factories in the same neighborhood as the kindergarten. For example, the Yu Yao Road Kindergarten which we visited in Shanghai—a medium-sized kindergarten serving 391 children—is under the direction of the neighborhood revolutionary committee. The kindergarten itself has a revolutionary committee of five members—two workers from the Mao Tse-tung propaganda team, one revolutionary cadre, and two teachers.

Institutions such as this one have been run by revolutionary committees only since the Cultural Revolution; before that, they were administered by people in the specific field. For example, a hospital would have been run by a hospital administrator, a factory by a

[17] Myrdal, p. 258.

manager, and a kindergarten by the head teacher. Because of the upheaval of the Cultural Revolution and the fear that a managerial elite was forming which was not sufficiently in contact with the workers, peasants, and soldiers, the administration of every institution was taken over by the sort of revolutionary committee we have described. Just about every institution in the society has had subsequently to undergo "struggle, criticism, and transformation" in order to evolve a working philosophy which would keep them in touch with the "mass." We were told at the Yu Yao Road Kindergarten that the two workers from the Mao Tse-tung propaganda team had entered the "superstructure" in order to participate in the process of struggle, criticism, and transformation that this institution was undergoing. They are workers from factories in the district, though they do not necessarily live in the district. The teachers on the revolutionary committee are recommended by the entire staff and then approved by "higher authority."

This "higher authority" is most likely the party branch committee, which actually makes the policy for the kindergarten; the kindergarten's revolutionary committee then carries out the policy. The party branch committee is made up solely of party members from the kindergarten—including all the staff, not just the teachers, but cadres and cleaning help as well.

This structure gives an idea of the importance of the Communist Party in basic decision-making and in insuring that the decisions are carried out. Over the party branch committee is the revolutionary committee of the street, which in turn is under the leadership of the Communist Party. Thus, at every level, the institution itself is run by a revolutionary committee, but that in turn is under the aegis of the party committee within the institution, and then up the line. This dual administrative system, by the units of the society and by the Communist Party, combined with the philosophy of Chairman Mao, which has been so widely disseminated through his writings, has made for a cohesion in the society and a similarity of goals which is most difficult to reproduce in any society not so constructed. This cohesiveness makes it possible for child-care institutions as with one voice to teach young children a unified value system that seemingly is accepted by all.

This does not mean that there is no conflict around the issues of how to implement policy or even what that policy should be. It is our understanding that such conflict does exist and indeed leads to endless discussions. And, of course, the Cultural Revolution demonstrated the conflict and dissension that can exist in China. Currently, in the early 1970's, however, it does seem that there is general consensus on major values and goals.

5

Multiple Mothering

For the ego, for the personality to develop, the infant needs to experience satisfaction and challenge at his own pace. But nowhere has it been demonstrated that for survival, or mental health the satisfactions, challenges, and frustrations must all originate in the same person.

BRUNO BETTELHEIM
The Children of the Dream

THE PEKING HANDICRAFT FACTORY IS COM-
prised of one large five-story building and a sprawling
set of workshops built around an open courtyard.
When we visited this factory, we wandered from workshop to workshop with our interpreter, Dr. Hsu, the secretary general of the Chinese Medical Association, Mr.
Hsu, and others in our party and watched women using
extraordinarily fine brushes to paint intricate pictures
on the inside of bottles about three inches high. We
also saw vases being fashioned by the elaborate process
of cloisonné. In another workshop, men and women
sitting on wooden stools were painting Chinese red de-
signs on black lacquer tables and cabinets; in a corner,
the master designer was teaching an apprentice new de-
signs for the furniture. They smiled as we watched
them but continued with their work. We saw jade and
ivory being carved so delicately that we felt we had to
tiptoe around the room lest we jar a worker's elbow.
We watched as traditional pictures were painted on
long strips of bamboo in lovely, muted colors.

Before 1949, we were told, this was all done by individuals working alone, with no guarantee that they
could make a living from their artistry. After Liberation, the workers were collected together in one place
and in 1952 formed cooperatives. The factory we vis-

ited was established in 1958 and the workers are entitled to all the benefits enjoyed by other factory workers.
Everything in the factory is hand-crafted; the goods are
made for sale to foreigners in China or for export.

One of the advantages for women working in the factory is that they can bring their newborn babies to the
factory's nursing room when they return to work after
maternity leave. The nursing room is upstairs on the
fourth floor of the large building here. When we visited
late one afternoon, there were twenty-seven babies in
the nursing room and four adults caring for them. This
visit to the nursing room was spontaneous, as were
many of our visits to other nurseries and kindergartens.
As we were being shown around the handicrafts factory,
we had asked if it had a nursery or a kindergarten.
When our hosts explained that they had a nursing
room in addition to a nursery-kindergarten combination, I asked to see the nursing room; a member of the
revolutionary committee, an interpreter, and I went
upstairs to visit right then. In much the same way, we
met the worker-doctor in one of the workshops; my
husband spotted a worker-doctor's medical bag, asked
to whom it belonged, and therein began an hour-long
conversation with the worker-doctor, who turned out to
be a charming and knowledgeable person.

The four adults in the nursing room—dressed in
white coats and called "Auntie" by the children—lost
none of their aplomb when I was shown in, asked many
questions, peered down at the very cute sleeping babies, taking notes all the while. The babies in this nursing room ranged from fifty-six days to a year and a half.
Most of the children seemed to be under eight months,
though there were a few babies about one year old in
playpens at the front of the room. The aunties corro-

borated that most mothers breast-feed their babies and come in twice during the day to do this; if the babies need more to eat, the aunties supplement with a bottle.

There were few toys in evidence, but the children who were awake were two to a playpen and two to a bamboo carriage, so they had each other for company. Some of the babies slept in cribs and some in carriages. When I asked what was done when the babies cried, I was told that they cannot be picked up, as there are too many; instead, the aunties wheel them back and forth in the carriages. Occasionally, however, they do pick one of the children up. The rather dark, dismal-looking room, painted as many of these rooms are, green from the floor to about halfway and white the rest of the way to the ceiling, was in direct contrast to the very pretty, multicolored clothes, supplied by the parents, that the children were wearing. The colorful quilts which covered each baby were also provided by the parents.

I wondered how the aunties were chosen. They told me that they were chosen from among the workers in the factory who are the "most responsible and the most patient." They have no special training.

Noticing the cement floor, nearly every square inch

"Auntie" and child in nursery, Shanghai

of which was covered with cribs, playpens, and carriages, I wondered if, as the children get older, they have an opportunity to walk around the nursing room. We were told that either they walk in a walker or the mother takes the child outside at lunchtime for a walk, but they do not walk on the floor, because it is "dirty." I had heard other aunties show the same concern over dirt and restrict children's mobility because of it. Here, as in other nurseries, they take the children's fingers out of their mouths because "their fingers are dirty." The children do not cry when their fingers are taken out of their mouths. And we saw no evidence of the use of pacifiers.

I took this opportunity, as I did several other times during our trip, to collect developmental data on very young children. The following developmental data, which are set forth in Figure 4, are a composite of con-

Figure 4

DEVELOPMENTAL DATA

Attends nursing room	56 days
Begins solid foods	5 months (if teeth)
Sits alone	6 months
Alternatively, may begin solid foods	7 months
Crawls	8 months
Stands alone	10–12 months
Begins to walk	1 year
Walks steadily	1½ years
Weaned to cup	1½ years
Begins to feed self with spoon	1½ years
Feeds self more steadily	2 years
Toilet-training	12–18 months
Speaks simple words	1½ years
Speaks sentences	1½–2 years
Eats with short chopsticks	3½ years

versations with several people involved in child-rearing; there was nearly always consensus on the ages of the various developmental stages. It is interesting to note that, according to ancient custom, the Chinese say a child is one year old at birth and celebrate a collective birthday (so much that they do is collective!) every year on New Year's Day. Thus, a child who is born in October becomes two years old on New Year's Day, which in 1972 was February 15, and adds a year every subsequent New Year. This form of reckoning ages began with the Chinese lunar calendar during the reign of Huang Ti around 2697 B.C. but was replaced by the Western calendar on January 1, 1912, by the Sun Yatsen government. Today nearly everyone, and certainly people working in the field of child care, uses the Western system of calculating age, but if one sees a small infant and is told he is a year old, one had better ask further.

Asking about motor development first, we were told that babies generally sit alone at about six months, crawl at around eight months, stand alone at from ten to twelve months, begin to walk at about one year, and walk more steadily by one and a half. Since I had been told by a Canadian living in China that Chinese children develop far more slowly than Western children and that Chinese mothers were aghast at the quick development of Western children, I made a point of asking at what age Chinese children walked. I was told everywhere that they generally walked at around one year; occasionally a little later. I corroborated this by noticing young children who seemed to be beginning to walk and asking their ages; invariably, they were around a year old. Interestingly, the motor development of Chinese children and of American children occurs at strikingly similar ages. However, the Chinese data are anecdotal and therefore the age estimates might be younger than if the data were systematically gathered.

Solid foods—noodles and porridge—are introduced at five months if the baby has a few teeth; if his teeth do not come in until later, he will start on solids at seven months. By a year and a half, too, the child can feed himself with a spoon, but it isn't until he is two that he can hold the bowl more steadily and feed himself with greater ease. All the children we saw eating were using small metal bowls and spoons, not chopsticks; when they are three and a half, they use a shorter version of chopsticks.

Toilet-training is collective and is begun at a year or a year and a half. From infancy until he is about eighteen months old, the baby wears diapers with a plastic covering, particularly at night. The most common sight, however, is the child with pants that open in the back—so he can squat to urinate or defecate when he needs to. And occasionally we saw small children do just this in the streets of Peking. Children wear open pants from the time they first wear trousers at around three months until they are from two and a half to three years old. Myrdal reports children wearing open pants in Liu Ling Village until they are six years old. Between twelve and eighteen months, the teachers begin toilet-training the children in the nursing rooms. After breakfast the children sit on white enamel potties and all have their bowel movements together! In another nursing room we visited, we were told that the children all sit on potties after lunch as well. Chinese children are expected to be trained by the age of eighteen months, but if they are not, the teachers in the nursery to which they go at a year and a half will help them. I did not have the feeling that toilet-training was an area of particular difficulty; adults were matter-of-fact when I talked with them about it and seemed to feel it was all fairly routine.

Children begin to speak simple words at between a year and a year and a half. In the nursing room of the Shanghai Machine Tool Plant, a factory famous for training workers to be engineers and technicians, there is a separate room for children twelve to eighteen months old. Half of the room was a sort of playpen in which the children could roam freely and play with toys, small dolls, paper flowers, a ball or two, that were more plentiful than in most other nursing rooms or nurseries. The teacher was in this play area with the children, and when we arrived, unannounced, she got them to sing to the accompaniment of an accordion. Clearly, these children were already speaking and singing. They also all walked. We were told at this nursing room that children begin to walk at ten months.

In the nursing room of the machine tool factory, fourteen adults were caring for sixty children, an astonishing ratio of one adult to every four children. This was the highest ratio of adults to children that we saw anywhere. This factory nursing room also had more varied equipment—individual playpens, rocking horses, toys, decorations on the walls and ceilings—but the structure of the rooms was similar to others; the floors and walls were cement, the rooms were generally dark, but with warm, smiling adults. The teachers were either junior or senior middle-school graduates with some knowledge of educational work. In addition to their training in education, they were given instruction in medical care by the factory's health center, so they

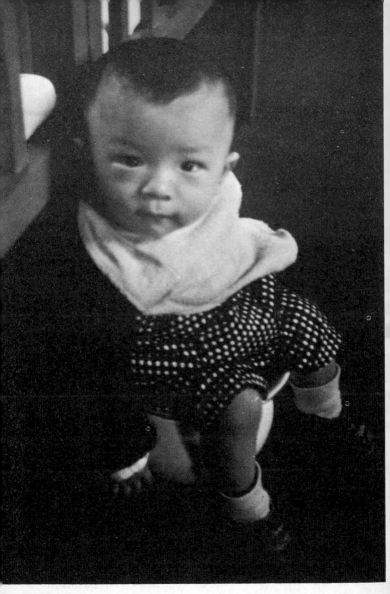

Toilet-training in the nursery of the Machine Tool Factory, Shanghai

Children in Machine Tool Factory nursery, Shanghai

could handle the "minor complaints" of the children.

As we have seen, children from a very young age receive multiple mothering—from the mother, while she is nursing, from the time the work day ends until it begins again the next day, and on her day off; from the several "aunties" in the nursing room, for they all care for all the children; and quite possibly from a grandmother who may live with the family. Bettleheim discusses the process whereby the infant must internalize both the satisfying and the frustrating aspects of mothering and points up the difficulties for the infant when the mothering figures are radically different from one another. As Bettleheim states with particular reference to the "collective upbringing" of the kibbutz in Israel, however, the adjustment to multiple mothering is made far easier for the infant when one strong central value system is held in common by the mother-figures.[1] This, as we have discussed in the previous chapter, is the case

[1] Bruno Bettelheim: *The Children of the Dream* (New York: Avon, 1970), p. 211–16.

Grandmother and grandchildren, Hangchow

in China today. Everyone we met seemed to hold similar values and to practice child-rearing in remarkably similar ways. This similarity was particularly striking to us as we are so accustomed to seeing a diversity of child-rearing patterns in the United States—from breast-feeding to bottle-feeding with a "propped" bottle; from constant use of a pacifier, sometimes until two or three years of age, to a forbidding of any extra sucking, pacifier or thumb; from toilet-training at ten months to training at three years; from the creation of a "child-proof" environment in which the child can wander freely to one in which a harness is used to control his every movement. Thus, China may be at one extreme of cohesiveness and American child-rearing at another extreme of diversity. Some of the implications of these differences will be discussed in a later chapter.

Another way of looking at "multiple mothering" or

Commune nursery, Shanghai

"shared mothering" is that infants can thrive physically and emotionally if the mother-surrogates are constant, warm, and giving. Babies in China are not subjected to serial mothering; we were repeatedly told that aunties and teachers rarely leave their jobs. And they are warm and loving with the children. The children show none of the lethargy or other intellectual, emotional, or physical problems of institutionalized children. Quite the opposite!

Not only are the mother-surrogates warm and loving, but so are the parents and grandparents. A word here might be helpful on the interaction between adults and children in general. During our wanderings in the cities and communes, we must have seen hundreds of adults with small children strolling along the streets looking at the National Day lights at night, walking through parks enjoying the sunshine and the brilliant red flowers set out for the holiday, hurrying to catch a bus to get to work, or shopping in large department stores or in small sidewalk shops. A few children who appeared to be less than a year old were pushed along the sidewalks in bamboo strollers, sometimes two strollers attached, with a baby in each of them. A more frequent sight, however, was mothers or fathers carrying babies asleep in their arms or strapped on their backs. Babies older than a year are likely to be carried in the parent's arms in a sitting position. The toddler most often walks between two adults, perhaps mother and father or parent and grandparent. The child's hand is held while he walks along or crosses the street; we rarely saw a child under seven or eight walking without some physical contact between adult and child.

And the children are remarkably well-behaved. Out of the several hundred children that we saw, we might

Babies in bamboo strollers

have seen three or four misbehave. They were surely on their best behavior when Americans were visiting their kindergartens, but this cannot account for the calm, relatively quiet, obedient, small-adult air of the children who were simply walking along the street. There just does not seem to be a battle going on between children and adults in the way that we know it. However, we were happy to see young boys doing cartwheels in Peking's Tien An Men Square!

We never saw an adult become angry with a child

while we were in China. We saw a few children cry, we even saw a few children misbehave, but this never occasioned anger in an adult. The adult spoke quietly to the child, patting him to reassure him, and indicating with a word or pressure of the hand or arm the direction his behavior or his body should take. Discipline was a combination of gentle admonition and encouragement: a pat on the shoulder and a smile combined to alter the behavior. In Peking, for example, we saw a small boy being carried on his mother's back pounding on her; the grandmother, who was walking beside them, gently patted his head and spoke to him quietly; he soon stopped. Coming out of a department store in Peking, we saw a girl perhaps five years old having what seemed to us to be a temper tantrum; her grandfather simply held her in his arms, standing in back of her as she stood on the sidewalk crying. The last we saw, her crying had subsided.

We have asked some Chinese-American students about the remarkably good behavior of Chinese children. In public, children are likely to be good, we were told, and parents would consider it a loss of face if they had to become angry in public. However, the students we spoke to all admitted to having been spanked in the privacy of their homes. We, of course, could not observe Chinese parents in their homes, except as visitors, which is a different thing.

Many people have asked us what has happened to the Chinese family since Liberation. Although the economic basis for the extended family has been eliminated by land reform, the family is still an important part of Chinese life and three generations frequently live together. The husband's mother has lost much of her former power, but the grandparents' role in child-rearing continues to be important. Before Liberation, the family was the individual's primary reference point, the central group he interacted with, the medium through which he learned about birth, death, religion, planting, and harvesting. Ideas were handed down within a family, scarcely questioned; and the individual's primary allegiance was to his family. Today the individual in China has multiple allegiances: to his family, his work, his Mao Tse-tung study group, his party branch, his local revolutionary committee, his city or commune, a set of ideas, and to China itself.

He is actively involved in groups on many levels. If he lives in the city, he may belong to groups at the factory and in the building or neighborhood where he lives; if he lives on a commune, he may be involved at the team, brigade, or commune level. This may be visualized as the individual being inside several circles which overlap and intersect to form a complex pattern. While the family still seems strong, other relationships are also important and many other influences now come to bear on the individual's thinking.

As the individual enters into multiple relationships all through his life, so does the infant start with multiple mothering in the nursing room, a beginning of the process of educating the new human being the Chinese are trying to fashion.

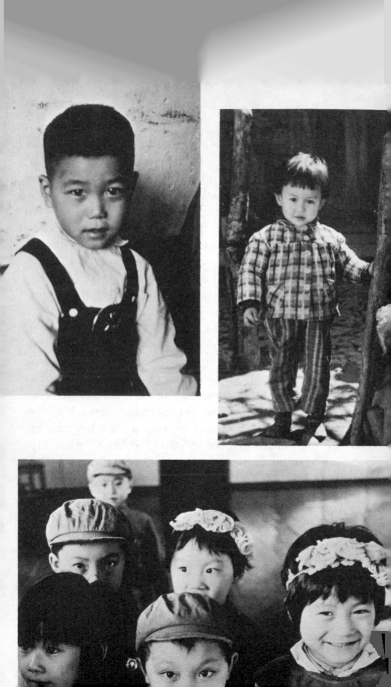

6

Learning to "Help Each Other" in the Nursery

> *When I am asked if the Chinese of today are happier than those of yesterday, there is at least one answer I can give with certainty. That is that the Chinese children have never been as happy as they are today; or as clean, as well dressed, and as well behaved; or as cheering a sight.*

ROBERT GUILLAIN
Dans trente ans la Chine

AS WE WERE LED INTO A CLASSROOM IN A WORK-ers' village, Chao Yang, in Shanghai, twenty-eight three-year-olds stood up and clapped excitedly for us. We sat in small chairs in the back of the room and watched as eight or nine of the children, seated on small chairs in the front of the room, chugged as though they were a train and sang for us a song about going on a train to Peking. They then reversed their position on the chairs and became horses as they were again riding to Peking. They finished their brief concert by gaily singing and dancing "Chairman Mao is our Great Savior," with the three teachers in the room tapping their feet and singing along with the children.

We were later told by Koo May-jun, a teacher in this nursery, that it takes children from the ages of one and a half to three and a half who live in Chao Yang. Chao Yang was built to house workers from the local textile factories and is made up of eight villages, as they are called. Each village has its own nursery to which the children can come after the nursing rooms in the factories. Comrade Koo said somewhat apologetically that this was only half-day care—from 6 a.m. to 6 p.m. However, if the parents have a meeting in the evening, the children can stay till 9 p.m. I interrupted to comment that that was a long day for a nursery to be open, I wondered if the teachers had to work such long hours. I was quickly reassured by Comrade Koo that the teachers work only an eight-hour-day; a teacher is not generally at the nursery all the time any given child is there.

I inquired if the children in the nursery were drinking from a cup by the time they arrived there and Comrade Koo indicated that they were. And in general they have been toilet-trained by the time they start in her nursery, as they have gotten their training in the nursing room "little by little." However, "some cannot manage their toilet habits and we have to help them. We cooperate with the parents, give the children hints, use the child's own words, and gradually build up their habits." She too, like Comrade Yung, felt that children who were cared for by their grandmother were often not trained by the time they started in the nursery; during their first month or two, they were trained here in the nursery.

Comrade Koo then described the following typical day (see Figure 5) at the nursery:

Cots for napping in Shanghai nursery

Figure 5

TYPICAL DAY   PART-TIME NURSERY
WORKERS' VILLAGE, CHAO YANG, SHANGHAI

6:00– 7:00 a.m.	Children brought to nursery
7:00– 8:30	Breakfast, games, free play
8:30	Gymnastics—outside when possible
9:00	Lecture
9:15	Snack—fruit
9:30	Outdoor activities, free play
10:15	Indoors, calm down, wash up
10:30–11:00	Lunch
11:00– 1:30	Sleep (one teacher on duty; the others have a rest)
2:00	Wake up
3:00	Snack, cakes
3:30	Games, organized by teacher (such as performances)
4:00	Outdoor play, free play
5:00	Supper

I wondered, of course, about the nine-o'clock lecture for one-and-a-half- to three-and-a-half-year-olds. Comrade Koo said that the format and content of the lecture very much depend on the age of the child. They try during that fifteen-minute period to teach some directives from Chairman Mao, "to have them armed with Chairman Mao's thought." The educational policy of the party, she reminded me, is to develop the child culturally, mentally, and physically, and various methods are used, including telling stories. This fifteen-minute period is also a time for military training.

Hearing about military training for a child this age led me to ask about aggression. Did some of the chil-

dren fight with each other, verbally or physically, I
wondered. According to Comrade Koo, some of the
children do quarrel, but the teachers educate them,
through Chairman Mao's thoughts, to love and help
each other, and care for one another. Generally they
understand and modify their behavior, but it does take
patience, Comrade Koo felt, and the teachers must re-
peat their words often to the children.

What is so amazing, of course, in walking the streets
of Peking or Shanghai, or visiting a commune or urban
neighborhood, is that we never saw aggression among
the children. No doubt it exists, but we never witnessed it. At one park in Hangchow, one of us handed
a piece of candy to a boy of about ten; he immediately
passed it on to his baby sister. He was then handed a
second piece, which he passed to his mother. He kept
the third piece; he had no one else to give it to.

Felix Greene noticed the same lack of aggression in
children during his trip.

> I have spent a lot of time watching children playing
> on the streets—little tots all on their own. They are
> endlessly inventive in their games—a piece of wood
> or a bit of string will keep them happy for hours.
> They never fight! *Why* don't they? They never snatch
> —never 'That's *mine!*' . . . They not only never fight
> but they *never* cry. The only child I have heard
> crying was one who was physically hurt." [1]

Knowing how important the concept of productive
labor is in child-rearing in China, I asked if the children do any "work." Comrade Koo said that the "work"
the children are taught at their age is how to take care

[1] Greene: *China,* p. 54.

of themselves. In the nursery they learn to dress themselves and to feed themselves; these tasks, it is felt, are enough at their age.

As in all the nurseries we visited, there was a small charge for the child's care, and the number of meals the child was to have at the nursery had to be arranged for in advance at extra cost. The child could come any time from six on, to fit in with the parents' working schedule, and leave any time from four on—that is, before or after supper.

Comrade Koo, who has children of her own, was formerly a factory worker. She left that job and attended night school in her spare time, attaining the level of a graduate of junior middle school. She then entered a training class sponsored by the Municipal Health Bureau and the Municipal Education Bureau for six months. This class involved both health work and education and prepared her for teaching in a nursery.

At the Institute for Biological Products the daily routine was very similar. In a class we visited of twenty three-year-olds there were two teachers. We came at lunchtime and were amazed to see a large pot of hot food on one of the small tables at which four children were sitting and eating. I wondered whether it was safe to leave a large, hot, full pot of food on the table so close to the children, but not one child touched it. This nursery is primarily a day nursery, though four children do spend the night when their parents are working on the night shift. They arrive any time after 7:30 in the morning and stay until 6:30 in the evening. Their routine includes Mao's quotes for a short period of time, some outdoor activity when the weather permits, singing, telling stories, lunch and nap, a snack (including fruit and tea), singing more songs, and then supper. On

Monday, Wednesday, and Friday the children study simple math; on Tuesday, Thursday, and Saturday they study Chinese characters. We were told that they have a bath once a week. The children eat all their meals at the nursery.

The brick building which housed the nursery had small areas of grass and trees in addition to an outdoor play area. The rooms were bright but the corridors were dark. There were the usual cement floors and walls, and no toys visible. But the quilts and the clothing the children wore were multicolored, the teachers wore white, and every child's face was solemn in wonderment at the Westerners invading their territory; we heard no crying. The three-year-olds napped on small cots and the two-year-olds in small cribs. The furniture was generally plain and functional, and as everywhere else in China, everything looked very clean. The teachers are family members of the workers at the Institute and receive a short period of training.

The nursery at the East Is Red (Dong Fang Hong) Hospital in Shanghai is typical of nurseries housed within work institutions. It is open twelve hours a day to all the employees of the hospital—doctors, nurses, auxiliary and cleaning help. Cribs are provided for the children to nap; meals are given them during the day; and they are cared for while their parents are working.

Still another nursery is run by the China Welfare Association, an organization founded in 1938 by Soong Ching Ling, the wife of Sun Yat-sen, and still headed by her. The association is supported by government funds and funds it itself raises. It is based in Shanghai and runs seven units: a maternity hospital, a full-time or twenty-four-hour-a-day nursery, a kindergarten, a youth palace (for children after school), an opera, a theater, and a children's journal. Yung Ping, a member of the nursery's revolutionary committee, described her nursery in some detail to me as we rode back and forth to places we visited in Shanghai. She is in her early forties and has three grown children. Though soft-spoken and somewhat self-effacing, she made every effort to obtain information for me and help me to understand pre-school care.

According to Comrade Yung, there are few full-time (twenty-four-hour) nurseries in Shanghai because of lack of facilities. She wishes that there were more, as children, she feels, progress more quickly in a nursery. At home, the children are "indulged in every respect by their grandparents," eat irregularly, are toilet-trained later, and in general develop more slowly. When I asked Comrade Yung if she felt that the children's being raised by grandparents fostered greater individualism and their being raised in a nursery led to greater collectivism, to their feeling more a part of the group, she vehemently agreed. Children who attend nurseries are "accustomed to mass activity," since they function mainly in a group. In a nursery, moreover, the child has "a regular life and regular activities, gets education, exercise, and training." All the people with whom we talked felt that more children should attend nurseries, but clearly the problem was one of resources. I wondered how children a year and a half react to being away from their parents twenty-four hours a day six days a week. "The first three months," Comrade Yung told me, "the children think about their parents, as they are not used to living apart from them. Sometimes after they have been home with their parents for a day and a

Lunchtime at the Institute for Biological Products, Peking

night they will come back in low spirits, but after a while they get used to living in the nursery and are not sad any more."

What about their relationship with their parents, since they spent so much time away from them? Comrade Yung felt that the relationship between parents and children is very close, partly because the children go home on the weekend or whatever day the parents have off from work. She pointed out that the parents work anyway and even if the child were home the parents would not be able to spend that much time with him. I wondered, thinking of our guide in Canton and her little girl, who lived at a twenty-four-hour-a-day nursery, how the child reacts at seven, assuming he has lived away from home at a twenty-four-hour nursery and kindergarten from the age of one and a half and then returns home to go to primary school. There were no boarding primary schools at the time, Comrade Yung told me, and at first the children are reluctant to leave the kindergarten and often come back to visit. But the children make a good adjustment once they return home to live, and since they have kept up a close relationship with their parents, they do not feel too strange at going back to live with them. Having the children live at home after age seven is not a problem since they are in

Nursery of the East Is Red Hospital, Shanghai

primary school six hours a day six days a week. Generally they come home for lunch, but one of the parents, who generally live near where they work, might be able to come home for lunch too, or the children can go to a neighborhood dining hall to eat.

The teachers who work at the China Welfare Association nursery have been trained in one of three ways: some are graduates of teachers schools; some have had a short period of training; and some have just been trained on the job. The schedule for a typical day in this nursery is given in Figure 6.

When I talked with Comrade Yung about the children's toilet-training, she corroborated what we had heard elsewhere—that after one or two months of using the potty at a specific time, the children got used to the schedule. However, they are not expected to be dry at night at the same age that they are expected to be trained during the day. At night the teacher routinely picks up the children and takes them to the bathroom —the one-and-a-half-year-olds twice during the night, and those over three once only. Thinking of the possibility of encouraging enuresis by bringing children to the bathroom while they are asleep, I asked if the children were awake when they were brought to the toilet or whether they were asleep. Comrade Yung said that the older children definitely were awake, and the younger ones half awake and half asleep. In spite of being brought to the bathroom twice during the night, 20 percent of the children from one to three years old still wet in bed; after age three, it was rare for them to do so.

As in the nursery in the workers' village, the nine-o'clock class in Mao Tse-tung thought included singing songs and telling stories with a revolutionary content.

Figure 6

TYPICAL DAY

FULL-TIME NURSERY, SHANGHAI

6:30 a.m.	Get up
7:00	Exercise, wash face with cold water
7:30	Breakfast
8:00– 8:30	Toilet, cultivate definite time
9:00– 9:15	Class in Mao Tse-tung thought
9:30–10:30	Outdoor activities—free play
10:30	Lunch—younger group first
11:30– 2:00	Nap
2:30	Get up
3:00	Snack: milk, biscuit, cakes, fruits for younger children; soybean milk for older group instead of milk, otherwise same
3:30	Organized play—games
4:00	Outdoor play—free play
5:00	Return to room—calm down
5:30	Dinner for the younger groups
5:45	Dinner for the older groups
6:45	Wash feet and get ready to sleep
7:30	Go to bed

For organized play at 3:30 in the afternoon, the children play such games as relay races, handing the red flag to one another as quickly as possible while standing in two rows. This not only passes on the red flag but trains muscles as well.

The goal in the nursery is to make sure that the children have ample time for free play but also to imbue them with collective principles. "Children like to move around a lot," Comrade Yung told us. "But they must learn to sit quietly at their lessons, to eat quietly in the dining room and to go to sleep. They learn that they have to raise their hand in class before they speak out. The teacher sets an example for the children; she sits in front of the children and keeps absolutely quiet until the children are quiet too. Being an example is more important than talking."

The children also learn collective principles from the Three Constantly Read Articles. They learn to "care for each other, love and help each other," through stories, pictures, and lantern slides, but most important they learn through actual activities. We were told repeatedly that if a child falls down, other children are taught to help him up. The teacher does not run to him but encourages the other children to go to him and help him. At the moment the child falls, the teacher says to the other children, "We have to help each other," and encourages them to do so right then. When I asked in some disbelief at what age the children would "help each other," she said that by three they were doing it. "At the beginning it is under the instruction of the teacher; but then it gets to be a habit. In the winter the children wear jackets with buttons up the back; since they cannot reach their own buttons, they button each other up; again they are encouraged to help each other."

But, I asked, aren't some children aggressive or hyperactive? What do you do with these children? Comrade Yung replied yes, some children are naughty. The teachers have decided that usually the naughty children are the most active children, those who like to work and like to learn to do physical labor, those who like to ask questions and are more clever than the others. "As

Chairman Mao says, we should divide everything into two parts; therefore, we should display the naughty child's good characteristics. If they like to move around a lot, we ask them to help the teacher. And since we have some children who are slow in understanding the lessons that the teacher is teaching, we ask the active ones, the naughty ones, to help the slower children. These techniques are usually tried with slightly older children—those from three years old on. Sometimes the teacher still has difficulty in dealing with naughty children, but she never gets angry." Having subjected Comrade Yung to a barrage of questions, some of which she must have thought quite strange, and never having seen her flinch, I can well believe that the teachers never get angry.

The idea of having the more active children use some of their energy to help the slower ones is not original to Comrade Yung's nursery. Partly because of the shortage of trained personnel, partly because of the therapeutic benefits of the helping role, and partly because it fits in with their ethic of "helping each other," the Chinese encourage unorthodox forms of mutual help. During the great literacy drive of the 1950's, kindergarten and primary-school children were taught to read in the schools and then sent home to teach their parents and grandparents. Members of the People's Liberation Army taught the peasants to read; each peasant then wore a Chinese character on his back for the peasant working behind him in the fields to learn. "Each one teach one" was the motto. Currently, in mental hospitals, patients are paired together, the healthier with the sicker, the ones who have been there longer with the new arrivals, to help them adjust, to help them understand their illness better. In medical schools we were told that "teacher teaches student, student teaches student, student teaches teacher."

The nurseries in the countryside are much simpler than those in the city. Often the entire nursery consists of one room, with little in the way of equipment. In the commune that we visited outside Shanghai, the nursing room and nursery were combined into one, with children from two months to four years attending. Usually there were six to ten children and two adults. This was a day nursery only, its purpose to free women to work in the commune. It occupied one room in a small cement building with little light coming in the small window. In a corner was a young mother nursing her baby while two other babies were being held by one of the teachers. The teachers have a very short period of training and then spend a half day a month in further training with personnel responsible for health and education in the commune. At this particular production team we were told that more children come to the nursery than stay with grandparents. Since there is no kindergarten, after age four the children have to be cared for by grandparents or by mothers who arrange to take care of each other's children.

At the Double Bridge Commune near Peking, each production team has its own nursery and kindergarten, which are open only during the day, from 7 a.m. until the end of the work day. The nursery takes children from a month to two years old, and the kindergarten from two to six years old. The nursery is staffed by a grandmother and the kindergarten by teachers recommended by commune members. These teachers have no special training but meet together to "exchange experiences." Their income is calculated, as is the income of other peasants, by the entire group, which decides how many work points the kindergarten staff should receive. The teachers are paid accordingly. Our host, Dr. Liu Jian, the thirty-six-year-old physician who was the responsible member of the "leading body" of the health center at the Double Bridge Commune, estimated that approximately 50 percent of the children were in the home, being cared for by grandmothers, and 50 percent were in the nursery.

At the Tea Brigade outside Hangchow, forty children from the ages of two to four attend a nursery which employs three teachers. The nursery is open only during the day; the number of children fluctuates depending on the season and how many mothers are needed to work in the fields. We were told that 60 to 70 percent of the families eligible send children to the nursery. It was in this nursery that we saw children—dressed in light blue smocks over their multicolored clothing, the girls with red ribbons in their hair—sitting at a long table stringing beads across the table, two by two, using

Stringing beads across the table, Hangchow

the same string. This activity seemed to be the height of cooperation for three-year-olds.

Our impression was that the nurseries in the urban areas were more concerned with teaching ideology than those on the communes, which seemed more like cooperative baby-sitting enterprises. In both locales, however, for this young age group, personnel are recruited far more on the basis of personality characteristics than of any kind of formal training, and we had the feeling that the Chinese consider a warm motherly type with common sense the best sort of person to care for small children. This anti-expert bias is, of course, reflective of what is going on in society at large.

Learning to live in a group the Chinese way involves a certain amount of regimentation (or, as some prefer to call it, orchestration) even at the youngest age. Many American viewers of television programs and movies depicting life in China have been dismayed by the sight of thirty small three-year-olds all getting up from their naps simultaneously, folding their quilts end to end in precisely the same manner, and marching down the street two by two. The Chinese do not see anything wrong with doing things together, in a prescribed way, and would feel that any other way would lead to chaos. Primary-school children walk down the street by twos; factory workers exercise together every morning; older students walk to the countryside to do "productive labor" in groups. For the Chinese have a saying, "If we are not as cement, we shall be as sand." "Sticking together" is clearly the Chinese way.

7

Learning to "Serve the People" in the Kindergarten

> *The world is yours, as well as ours, but in the last analysis, it is yours. You young people, full of vigor and vitality, are in the bloom of life, like the sun at 8 or 9 in the morning. Our hope is placed on you. . . .*
>
> *The world belongs to you. China's future belongs to you.*
>
> MAO TSE-TUNG, 1957

A GROUP OF FIVE-YEAR-OLDS COME DANCING into a large, bare, sunlit room singing, "I have a colored pencil," and "With a red pencil I will draw a red flag and with a black pencil I will draw a map of Africa." Accompanied by a teacher playing the accordion, and using broad gestures, they act out the song gaily. Another group dances in singing a current popular song: "It is ridiculous to have two Chinas; we are determined to liberate Taiwan!" With fierce expressions on their faces and fists raised in revolutionary determination, the children sing, "The poor people of the world must win victories."

These are children of the Pai Hai Kindergarten, a "full-time" kindergarten situated in a lovely park in Peking. They are putting on a typical performance for American visitors, with the usual aplomb, cheeriness, and lack of self-consciousness that we saw everywhere. The Pai Hai or North Sea Kindergarten, which is run by the city of Peking, was founded in 1949 for children from ages three and a half to seven. Three hundred and ninety children, divided into fifteen classes, were enrolled. Each class had three teachers. With a total of forty-nine teachers, the kindergarten had a ratio of one teacher to every eight children. This was one of the highest ratios of teachers to children that we encoun-

Pai Hai Kindergarten, Peking

tered. As a twenty-four-hour kindergarten, Pai Hai needed, of course, a greater number of teachers to children. In twelve-hour-a-day kindergartens, the ratio was more often one teacher to every thirteen to fifteen children.

Pai Hai is probably the most beautiful kindergarten we saw in China. Its architecture is a combination of traditional Oriental and functional modern. The buildings are built around a central playground bordered by flowering plants, and the small young trees that are planted all over Peking dot the playground. As is usual in Peking, a dust-like substance covers the ground, for it is very difficult to grow grass here. In addition to the trees and plants, the playground contains swings, two jungle gyms, three slides, a seesaw, a sandbox, and several benches. Children spend six days a week twenty-four hours a day at Pai Hai, usually going home on Saturday afternoon and returning on Monday morning; the kindergarten is open all year around except for holidays. Sick children are kept at the kindergarten in a ward that is attended by two physicians, and there is a clinic as well. The plan for a typical day at Pai Hai is given in Figure 7.

Figure 7

A TYPICAL DAY
PAI HAI KINDERGARTEN, PEKING

7:00 a.m.	Get up. Children dress themselves, fold quilt. Morning exercises, clean bedroom and classroom, wash up
8:00	Breakfast
8:30– 9:00	Free time
9:00	Classes: junior group, only one class; middle and older group, two classes
10:00	Exercises, walk along the river
11:45–12:30	Lunch
1:00– 3:00	Nap in the summer
1:00– 2:30	Nap in the winter
After nap	Snack: fruit and a sweet
3:00	Class for middle and senior groups. Stories, exercises, and practicing performances
4:00– 5:30	Outdoors—free play
6:00	Supper—wash up, a bath (summer)
7:00	Television or lantern slides or outdoors for a walk
8:00	Bedtime in winter
9:00	Bedtime in summer

The children nap longer in the summertime because it is hot and they are being protected from the heat; in the winter they nap for a shorter time so they will not miss the sun. They generally sleep during their nap times and do not give the teachers any difficulty. They are divided by age for sleeping, not by sex—that is, boys and girls live together until age seven. And as in all other kindergartens and nurseries in China, their only personal possessions are their clothing and quilts.

The children's sleeping quarters, their bathroom, and their classroom are all side by side, so that each group of children lives in a relatively small, self-contained part of the school. The children's bathroom has small white sinks and small cubbyholes for their towels. Their sleeping room is one large sunny room, filled with wooden cribs, one right next to the other. The

Bedroom in the Pai Hai Kindergarten

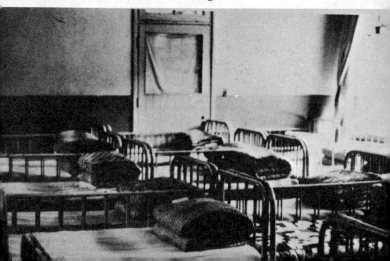

cribs have a quilt folded up at the foot of each one. Next to each sleeping room is a classroom, whose walls, as in other classrooms we saw, are painted half green and half white. As in the nurseries, there are very few toys in evidence, although on bookcases in some of the classrooms small dolls are displayed which represent the various occupations in China: a soldier, a barefoot doctor, a member of the People's Liberation Army, a school child, a factory worker, a guerrilla fighter, a member of a propaganda team, a peasant, and a female member of the militia. Two or three posters usually hang on the walls, always including one of Mao.

There is no evidence in Chinese nurseries or kindergartens of mechanical toys, blocks or other building equipment, stuffed animals or live animals. Interestingly, the Chinese are manufacturing many of these kinds of toys. We saw elaborate mechanical cars, soldiers, and other gadgets both at the Shanghai Industrial Exhibition and for sale in department stores, but these items are obviously for export or for personal consumption, not for use in day-care facilities. This paucity of

Children's bathroom, Pai Hai Kindergarten

equipment adds to the impression that teaching and learning in China are a people-to-people phenomenon.

Of the seven classes we visited at Pai Hai, four of them demonstrated specific teaching techniques used by the teachers, and the children put on performances in the other three. In the drawing class for five-year-olds, the children were sitting at their desks drawing pictures with crayons. They were drawing Tien An Men Square in Peking, the sun rising in the East, Mao's birthplace, or mountains with a red flag on top. Each child selected his own topic, but all the pictures were revolutionary in content.

We visited a slide show for six-year-olds in which twenty-two children sitting quietly in rows on small chairs with their hands in their laps were listening to a teacher animatedly tell the story of Norman Bethune while another teacher projected slides. As she told Bethune's life, the teacher occasionally asked the children a question, and they would answer either in unison or she would call on a specific child. She pointed out that Bethune himself made the medical tools which he needed to perform surgery and that this was an example of "self-reliance" and "selflessness." When the slides were finished, she asked the children what they had learned.

One child: "The spirit of mutual help."

Another child: "To think of others first—then ourselves."

"How he treated the patients and only cared about them, not himself, and how he mixed with the mass."

"How he donated his own blood to help his patients."

The teacher could not call on the children as quickly as they wanted to speak. At the very end she asked, "If you were to find a child sick on the street, what would you do?" The child's response: "I would get medicine for him and water for him." We were interested that the child did not say he would go find a doctor or his mother.

Twenty-six six-year-olds were sitting in rows by twos, with one teacher at the head of the room by the blackboard. There was more equipment in this room; there were small blocks out of which one could form six different pictures by turning the blocks. All six pictures were military in theme and showed such scenes as a female member of the People's Liberation Army throwing a hand grenade, a schoolboy bayoneting a stick figure of a "foreign devil," or a barefoot doctor running to care for the wounded. There were also many books in comic-book form, with action-filled pictures and narrative at the bottom of the page, which are used as readers. The subjects included a young guerrilla fighting the Japanese, a biography of Lenin, an army doctor heroically caring for her patients, and a peasant, hurt in the war, who recovers and becomes a leader of his commune.

Kindergarten readers

The teacher tells the children how the Young Pioneers use their Sundays to help the commune. They collect four wheelbarrows of manure in the morning and five wheelbarrows in the afternoon. How many have they collected in all? The teacher is simultaneously using small cardboard wheelbarrows as visual aids pinned up on a chart. As she is talking, she puts up four and then five more, pointing out the nine at the end. She does the same with each example. "A group of Youth Pioneers raised four black pigs, and then they raised six more. How many pigs have they raised in all?" Nearly all the hands go up. "They have collected three bushels of wheat," says the teacher as she pins up three cardboard pictures of wheat, "and then they collect seven more bushels. How many have they collected in all?"

Throughout the arithmetic lesson the children have been attentive, paying little attention to the Western visitors in the back of the room. All the answers are correct; it is clear they know this arithmetic lesson.

In the classroom next door, twenty six-and-a-half-year-olds are learning to write Chinese characters. The word being taught is "unite," as in "Unite to win still greater victories," a quotation from Chairman Mao. The quotation is written at the top of the blackboard in red chalk and underneath it the teacher writes the character for "unite" very slowly on the board, calling out the order of the strokes in unison with the children. When she asks for volunteers to come up to the blackboard to try to write it, many hands shoot up. She calls on two boys. One evidently writes it correctly. She corrects the slight mistake the other child made, patting him on the shoulder, and then turns to the rest of the class and says, "Is it correct?" "Correct!" the rest of the

Arithmetic class, Pai Hai Kindergarten

children shout together. The two boys return to their seats, smiling.

When we were ready to leave Pai Hai Kindergarten after having visited the classes, we walked out of the last classroom and saw a bandstand set up with perhaps half a dozen chairs in front of it. The children streamed out of the classrooms and took seats to the right of the bandstand. We took our seats in front and were then treated to a polished, enthusiastic performance of seven or eight "numbers." The children who were not participating on the stage in any given song sat at their places and played a musical accompaniment on drums, tambourines, cymbals, or Chinese traditional wooden instruments, and sang along. One or two of the teachers sat with them and sang also, and a couple of others stood in the background, watching. Halfway through the performance, we watched happily as one boy pushed another boy's P.L.A. hat off. The second boy put it back on. When it happened again, one of the teachers went and sat beside the mischievous one, laughing, put her arm around him and whispered a few words in his ear. It didn't happen again.

After the performance, we again spoke with some of the teachers. We learned that the children address teachers by their family name plus "Laoshi," the word for teacher. Many of the teachers have been at Pai Hai for as long as twenty years. The average salary is fifty yuan a month, the pay scale ranging from forty to eighty yuan a month, the same as a typical factory worker's salary. We wondered what a teacher would do if she was not happy there, and after some perplexity on the part of our hosts, we were told that all the teachers came voluntarily and that they were never unhappy there. This may be hard for the Westerner to believe, but it is what we were told.

The cost for a child to live at Pai Hai is 20.20 yuan a month, which includes eight yuan for food. This is a substantial part of a worker's income, though if a child is at such a kindergarten, the family undoubtedly has two incomes. If the family cannot pay the entire cost, the factory the parents works at will pay part. For comparison, we thought of Comrade Chen in Canton, who pays twelve yuan a month for her little girl's twenty-four-hour nursery.

We left Pai Hai late in the afternoon as the sun was going down and the air becoming chilly. The children crowded around our cars and clapped and waved the paper flowers they had used in their singing. We clapped, waved back, and were sorry to leave.

At the Yu Yao Road Kindergarten, in Shanghai, we were greeted by a flood of children running toward us, saying: "Welcome, Uncle and Auntie!" A child had evidently been assigned to each of us. My friend was Pan Yun, six years old, who had a pixie-like face, with light pink lipstick on because she was to perform, and short glossy hair, and who wore a black velvet, embroidered vest over her blouse and skirt. Vic's small host, Sun Guo-youn, four years old, was dressed in a white shirt and blue overalls, with a big red Mao button in the center of his overalls. He was a beautiful, sober, round-faced little boy who obviously didn't know exactly what to make of the situation. At one point Vic set him on his lap, and though obviously not comfortable, he put up with it nicely.

This was the first kindergarten where students were present during our talks before and after we were shown around the premises. We sat at the traditional long conference table drinking tea and our little hosts sat beside us, never fidgeting or fussing. Comrade Gao, a striking-looking woman in her thirties with a mobile, laughing face, the representative of the teachers, told us that since the parents are almost always at their own jobs, the teachers feel they must do an especially good job so that the parents can "work harder and grasp the revolution." "Children are educated to be loyal to Chairman Mao, the Communist Party of China, internationalism, and patriotism," Miss Gao told us. "They are trained to love heroes, to love the workers, peasants, and soldiers, and to take part in physical labor in order to love physical labor from the earliest stage." She felt that the educational transformation was in process, but

the ideological remolding of teachers was lagging behind. We asked about the retraining of teachers since
the Cultural Revolution. If the changes resulting from
the Cultural Revolution were as great as indicated, then
teachers would need new guidelines to reorganize their
own thinking and teaching. Miss Gao felt that the retraining of teachers was "necessary and urgent" because
they have to "remold their world outlook." However,
most of the retraining must be done by the teachers
themselves, as this has not, for the most part, been organized by the district. She linked studying Chairman
Mao's thought to the concept of "self-reliance" and indicated that this was each teacher's responsibility. The
teachers also have to study their professional work in
order to make up stories and design dances appropriate
to the goals of the post-Cultural Revolution period. Occasionally the city government organizes training classes
which teachers attend; occasionally they exchange experiences with teachers from other schools; but most of
the work is done on their own.

We were invited to visit some of the classrooms; the
first was a class in Mao Tse-tung thought. Twenty-nine
five-year-olds were sitting in a semicircle listening to a
small, vivacious woman in her early thirties tell the
story of a model teacher in a commune who studies the
works of Chairman Mao so well that she is chosen to go
to National Day in Peking.

Teacher: "What would you say to Chairman Mao?"
One child: "We are thinking of you day and night."
Another child: "All of us are longing for you."
Teacher: "The teacher went to Peking. What trans-
portation would she use?"
In unison: "A train."
"She studies on the train and sings songs. The other

Comrade Gao, teacher in the Yu Yao Road Kindergarten, Shanghai

Mao Tse-tung thought class for five-year-olds

passengers sing songs, too. The workers kept the train going very well because representatives of the workers, peasants, and soldiers were on the train. Where will the teacher live in Peking?"

"Where the leaders live."

"The model teacher is moved to tears. Why? Because the workers and peasants were opposed by the landlords, and only after Liberation did they have a good life. Every family of poor and lower-middle peasants had a bad history before Liberation. The model teacher had only a father, because all the others in her family had died. Her father couldn't afford to pay rent on his land and the landlord put him into prison. Therefore, the teacher is moved to tears because she will now be staying where the leaders stay and her life is so different now."

Teacher: "October 1—what is it?"

"National Day!" the children shout.

"I can't hear you!"

"National Day!" they shout louder, with glee.

With a downward motion of her hands, she calms them. "The representatives can't sleep because tomorrow they are going to see Chairman Mao. The next morning, where are they going?"

"Tien An Men."

She uncovers the easel next to her and shows a poster of workers, peasants, and soldiers cheering and waving their red books, a red flag in the background and a banner with Chinese characters in the foreground. The teacher applauds the parade and asks the children what they see in the picture.

"Long live Chairman Mao!" (The writing on the banner.)

"What else do you see?"

"Long live Chairman Mao!"

"Red flags flying."

The teacher points out the model teacher in the picture and says with great feeling, "One moment later she will see Chairman Mao and she is very excited." (The children are now getting more and more excited themselves and can hardly stay in their seats.) "What will they sing?"

"The East Is Red."

The teacher uncovers another picture and it is of Chairman Mao, applauding. The teacher and the children shout, "Long live Chairman Mao!" with arms raised.

"Who is the dearest to us?"

"Chairman Mao!"

She quiets them with a downward motion of her hands. They all then stand at their chairs and sing and dance about loving Chairman Mao, the teacher doing the same dance steps and gestures in front of the room.

The class for five-year-olds in Mao Tse-tung thought ends.

We were then led by our student hosts to a class in revolutionary art and culture. Twenty-four five-year-olds are sitting four to a desk. A picture of an ocean liner is pinned on the blackboard and on the picture are Chinese characters which say: (1) Keep initiative in our own hands. (2) Self-reliance. (3) This ocean liner was made by the Chinese working class. The children stand by their desks and sing and clap out a song about the building of the boat. The teacher then tells the story of the making of the ocean liner: "It was made by the working class. Before Liberation we could not make ocean liners, but after Chairman Mao's decree that 'we should rely on ourselves,' the working class answered Chairman Mao's policy actively by building the liner. The ocean liner can carry cargo to many parts of the country; it can carry friendship to other countries; and the little Red Guards will take the liner to other countries to learn more." The teacher then draws on the blackboard a simplified picture of the ocean liner in yellow, blue, and pink chalk, at the same time describing how she is drawing it. She asks them to draw the same kind of boat using their colored pencils and their drawing books. While the teacher was telling the story about the boat, one child kept peeking around to look at the visitors. Finally the child behind her poked her in the back, and she faced front immediately.

Next we visited a class in productive labor in which twenty-six children from ages four to five sat at two long tables folding small crayon boxes. We immediately thought that this was "make work" and asked our interpreters to find out from the teacher why they were folding the boxes. We learned that the boxes of crayons are made for export, and indeed the writing on one side is in Chinese and on the other in English: "Great Wall Wax Crayons, Shanghai, China." This "productive labor" is work that would have to be done by factory workers if the children did not do it. The factory leases the work to the kindergarten and then pays the kindergarten according to the number of boxes folded. The money is used to purchase extra equipment, such as a television set, for the children. The children do "productive labor" during one period a week, sometimes for thirty minutes, sometimes for fifty minutes. When they are not folding boxes, they occasionally wrap crayons and put them in the boxes. They sit quietly and fold the boxes, putting them in piles in front of them on the table. Periodically the teacher gathers up the boxes and puts them in a large basket in the middle of the room. There is no competition to see who can fold the most boxes; they do not hurry through, making a game of it; they simply sit there and fold. As we were about to leave the classroom to go on to another one, they stood

Productive labor, Shanghai Kindergarten

up and sang us a song, clapping out the beat, about how they love physical labor and will go to the country-side to work.

We were then treated to one of the best perfor-mances we saw. After we returned to the conference table and more hot tea, a group of boys and girls rang-ing in age from three and a half to six and a half danced out, pretending with the aid of tambourines, bells, and a lively piano played by one of the teachers that they were members of a propaganda team. The girls were wearing clothes similar to my little friend Pan Yun's clothes—black velvet embroidered vests, skirts, and pink or red ribbons in their hair. Gaily they sang, "The Chinese Communist Party is leading the cause forward, and Leninism is leading the cause for-ward." No teacher seemed to be directing them, just a small announcer, who "warmly welcomed their Ameri-can friends" and announced each song. Eight three-and-a-half-year-olds marched out carrying sticks that substituted for guns, and in a determined tone of voice sang, "We must heighten our vigilance to defend the Motherland." As usual, all the children sang every song, not just the children who were performing. The tunes were fast and catchy, and dramatic acting was in-volved in the songs and dances.

A group of boys came out in blue overalls and white shirts, including our friend, Sun Guo-youn, looking just as cheerful and at ease on the stage as he looked slightly bewildered and solemn sitting next to us at the table. One boy had a hammer, one a scythe, and one a gun, as they acted out the roles of worker, peasant, and soldier and sang that they wished Chairman Mao a long, long life. "Stars are twinkling in the sky, too many to be counted; but the brightest one is in Peking." Then, speaking in unison, "I love Peking because I see Chairman Mao." Immediately seven more children with chartreuse paper flowers came out to continue the song at an even faster pace, waving their flowers. Finally, little Red Guards skipped in with small red school bags. They sang how they go to school with a treasure. "Do you know what the treasure is? I know! It's Chairman Mao's quotations!" (A teacher offstage beat out the rhythm of this song with a traditional wooden instrument.) The children had gotten out the little red books from the little red school bags to show the treasure; one girl dropped her book but continued her performance without missing a beat, only occasionally glancing down to the floor where the book was. Just before they danced out, a male employee of the kindergarten picked it up and handed it to her., Then they ran offstage, putting the books back into the bags and waving goodbye.

The Yu Yao Road Kindergarten is open to all children in the neighborhood. When we visited, 391 children were enrolled, ranging in age from three and a half to six and a half. There were thirty-one staff members and the children were divided into twelve classes, so each class had roughly thirty-two or thirty-three children, and there was a ratio of approximately one teacher to every thirteen children. We did not see a class of more than thirty children, probably because some were home ill.

We asked if there were retarded children at this kindergarten and were told that in general there aren't. Sometimes children attend whose mental development is not as good as that of the rest, but they usually catch up. If the teachers find this to be the case with a child, they communicate with the parents. However, they con-

Singing and dancing in the Yu Yao Road Kindergarten, Shanghai

sider that it is their "main duty," not that of the parents, to help the child catch up.

We were particularly impressed with how hard the teachers worked here and at the other kindergartens. Obviously, our being there made the entire morning one large performance. Nevertheless, I have rarely seen a teacher in the United States or in the other countries I've visited make such efforts to communicate with the children as all the teachers seemed to in this kindergarten. One of the favorite words of the Chinese is "whole-heartedly"; it is an apt description of the teaching we saw there.

A further word on physical labor. As these children folded boxes, so did children in other kindergartens do productive labor. At Pai Hai they wipe off the tables in their rooms, sweep the floor, plant seeds, and grow vegetables. The teachers felt that if the children participate in the growing process and understand it, they will have greater respect for the peasants, will understand how things grow, and will eat better because they will realize all the work that goes into growing their food.

We were also very interested in the emphasis on militarism. The children do march like soldiers, carrying sticks, which they use as though they were guns, and as the workers and peasants are glorified, so are the soldiers. And of the few toys we saw, many of them were military in nature. The emphasis on the People's Liberation Army and on defending the motherland stands in sharp contrast, however, to the lack of aggression you see in the children in their day-to-day life. That we never saw a child push another child, never saw a child grab a toy from another child, never saw any hostile interaction between children or between adults and children truly amazed us. When we asked about aggression at a kindergarten at the workers' village in Shanghai, we were told by the kindergarten teacher, Lu Shiu-tsung, that aggression is not a problem, because the children have already "received collective training in nursery." She allowed that occasionally a child might be aggressive, but this usually can be handled through "education."

A typical day at the Workers' Village Kindergarten is seen in Figure 8.

Figure 8

A TYPICAL KINDERGARTEN DAY
WORKERS' VILLAGE, CHAO YANG, SHANGHAI

7:00– 8:30 a.m.	Parents bring children. Free play Breakfast, light labor (clean table, chairs, brush floor, pick up "wastes" in garden, and wash own towel)
8:30	Outdoor gymnastics
9:00– 9:30	Class for study of Chairman Mao's works
9:30– 9:40	Little rest
9:40–10:10	Second class: revolutionary art and culture
10:10–11:10	Outdoor activities
11:10–12:30	Lunch
12:30– 2:45	Nap
2:45– 3:15	Get up, fold blanket, snack
3:15– 3:30	Read Chairman Mao ("daily reading period")
3:30– 4:30	Indoor activities, books, pictures, ping-pong, radio
4:30	Dinner

We talked at some length about the classes for the study of Chairman Mao's works. Comrade Lu told us that the class may take any of several forms. The teacher may tell the children a story which illustrates why they should love the People's Liberation Army, or they may look at pictures and tell a story about them. A "veteran worker" might be asked to tell stories of the "bitter past," to contrast it with the present; there is great concern that the children who have never known the "bitter past" understand something of what life used to be like.

A kindergarten in Hangchow

In the class for revolutionary art and culture, the children might sing revolutionary songs, play games, or learn to play simple musical instruments. The children were listening to the radio late in the afternoon and Comrade Lu said that there was a special youth broadcast that was on at certain times during the day for children in kindergarten.

In the brief fifteen-minute "daily reading period," the teacher reads a quote from Chairman Mao and the children listen. Sometimes the teacher chooses specific quotes that relate to what may have gone on in class during the day. Thinking of our children's books, I wondered if the government had put out an edition of Chairman Mao's thoughts especially designed for children, with large characters and pictures. It took them some time even to understand what I was asking and then they vigorously shook their heads and said, "Oh, no, the children are not supposed to learn the characters in studying Mao's thoughts; they are just meant to understand the meaning." They don't use the book itself in studying the thoughts. The teacher simply says them out and they discuss the meaning. Comrade Lu made it clear that though the children carry the little red book, they are in no way expected to be able to read it; it is merely a "sign of loyalty."

However, by the time the children have finished kindergarten, they can read a little. They can read "Long live Chairman Mao," "Long live our Communist Party," and as we saw in Pai Hai, "Unite to win still greater victories." They can do simple addition from one to ten and can write simple characters. When they start primary school, they are going into what might be equivalent to our second grade.

It seemed to us that the girls were more proficient in the performances than the boys were, and we wondered if girls were ahead of the boys in development, but Comrade Lu felt that they were at the same level; girls simply perform better because "they enjoy the dancing more."

Two of the songs we heard at the Workers' Village Kindergarten, which are often sung during performances, can help clarify the current role of women as acted out by the children. In the first song, eight girls in blue shorts and white blouses danced into the room waving red flags and cardboard sabers and acted out a scene from the revolutionary ballet "The Red Detachment of Women," in which women are portrayed as fine soldiers committed to the revolutionary cause. The plot concerns a peasant girl from the island of Hainan who is beaten by the landlord's henchmen and left, hurt, in the forest. She is found by a detachment of revolutionaries, mainly women, and the remainder of the story tells of her maturing as a member of the detachment and their revenge on the landlord. The other song sung by the children and frequently heard is from "The White-Haired Girl"—the scene in which male soldiers from the People's Liberation Army free a village and girls from the village offer the soldiers food and presents, indicating, as our interpreter told us, "the close relationship between the people and the army." These two views of women—fierce, militant, equal to men, on the one hand, and traditional, food-preparing, morale-giving supporter at home, on the other—are reflective of the society's larger view. And it is quite appropriate that children act out the larger society's views of the role of women, as they do in other areas.

For one of the most striking aspects of the teaching of pre-school children in China is that the values, ideas, and premises of the larger society are handed down to them in toto, without diluting or sugar-coating. Children are considered citizens today as well as in the future, and this is a time of preparation for their role as full-fledged citizens when they are older students, teenagers, and adults. Though some aspects, such as militarism, may be jarring to Western visitors, the attitudes of protecting the motherland, defending the country against war, supporting third-world nations in spirit, and the determination to liberate Taiwan are directly reflective of China's current policies and are therefore part of the children's education.

Women's militia from "The Red Detachment of Women"

Welcoming the soldiers, from "The White-Haired Girl"

8

Israel, the Soviet Union, and China: Some Similarities and Some Differences

> . . . *An active and conscious member of his kibbutz [should be]* . . . *devoted to his People, and versed in its history; faithful to his homeland and prepared to defend it; devoted to the workers' movement, the socialist nations and the concept of brotherhood among peoples; expert in the problems of the country and of the world, and alert to what is happening in them; at home in the concepts of the scientific world; and of cultivated esthetic taste.*

> An educational theorist,
> the Kibbutz Federation

> *It is particularly important that a boy's or girl's feeling of solidarity should not be based only on the narrow pattern of the family; it should extend beyond the boundaries of the family into the broad sphere of Soviet life and the life of mankind in general.*

> A. S. MAKARENKO
> A Book for Parents

IN EXAMINING CHILD-REARING PATTERNS IN China, and particularly while listening to descriptions of the kind of human being the Chinese are trying to fashion, one cannot help but think of other societies with similar goals and methods. The system of child care of many countries—the Scandinavian countries, the nations of Eastern Europe—might be compared to what we observed in China, but I have chosen for comparison two countries that I find particularly fascinating, Israel and the Soviet Union.

The Soviet Union, several of whose child-care facilities we visited in the summer of 1967, has been, of course, a pioneer both in the area of child care and in the liberation of women. After Liberation in 1949, the Chinese modeled many of their services on Soviet patterns with the help of Soviet advisors and technicians. As the rift grew between the two countries, the Chinese have gone more and more their own way, developing institutions which are based on their cultural heritage, their needs and problems, and which are responsive to the brand of Communism they are evolving. Thus, the comparison of Chinese and Soviet child care is valuable in understanding the goals of the two societies.

The kibbutz in Israel has been a major pioneering effort in redefining the role of women and of the family and experimenting with new ways of caring for children. The philosophy, goals, and methods of child-rearing in the kibbutz seemed, therefore, a likely area for exploration and comparison.

There are striking similarities as well as marked differences in the child-rearing methods used in the kibbutz of Israel, in the nursery schools (yasli) and kindergartens (detsky sad) of the Soviet Union, and in the public child-care facilities in China. Although there are differences within each system, from kibbutz to kibbutz in Israel and from city to countryside both in the Soviet Union and in China, there is a general consensus of goals within each society which affect child-rearing patterns.

In the Soviet Union it has been reported that 40 percent of children in the cities attend the yasli, and 80 percent of the children in the cities attend the detsky sad. As in China, there is a small fee for sending a child to a nursery or kindergarten, and this is calculated according to a fee scale. A child attends the yasli from the age of two months, after the end of maternity leave, to three years, and the kindergarten from three years to six years; the child enters primary school at age seven. As in China, the nursery or kindergarten may be simply a day school, or it may be a five-day school, with the children spending their weekends at home. There are far fewer of this latter type because of the great expense involved in making them available. Again as in China, nursing mothers are encouraged to bring their children to the nursery where they work and are given time off to nurse the infants and to play with them. Some kindergartens are attached to factories and farms, and some are in the neighborhoods in which the families live.

During the first year of life in a Soviet nursery, a

great deal of attention is paid to developing the children's sensory-motor function and their language ability. The Soviets have what they call a "regime," in which the child is stimulated regularly by brightly colored toys and his limbs are exercised rhythmically by the nurse. Their senses are thus stimulated in an effort to hasten their development. Through play, children are further stimulated to advance through each stage of development in the yasli from crawling to standing to walking. They are methodically encouraged by warm, loving teachers who follow a plan laid out by the pre-school institute. The teachers know at what age children should be able to roll a ball, climb, take short walks, and play with special toys geared to aid their development. As the child learns to master games, new ones are substituted. The kindergarten and the nursery are thought of as collectives, just as the family is thought of as a collective, and the children are taught to consider themselves part of the collective. There is, nevertheless, a good deal of individual instruction in addition to group instruction.

Much attention is paid in the Soviet Union to holding the child's interest; one visitor noted that she found very little boredom in the Soviet nurseries and kindergartens. The Soviet pre-school system is based on the assumption that the child should perform to the limit of his ability; the teachers give tasks to be performed which will take the length of time of his attention span. Thus, they attempt not to ask of the child any more than he can do but to expect from him all he can do. Pavlov's theories of conditioning are, of course, of vital importance in the Soviet theories on conditioning the child to develop both his abilities and his self-control. This bears a striking similarity to the Chinese experience with both children and adults. In both the medical and the educational fields we were struck by the fact that adults were expected to perform to the limit of their ability, were trained up to the job they needed to do, and were very rarely overtrained.

An interesting difference between the Soviet and the Chinese system of education for young people is the Soviet use of non-political and non-revolutionary materials such as books, toys, songs, and games. In learning to paint, the Soviet child may well paint a tree or a flower with no political meaning; in music he may sing a song about "Grandfather Frost," or "Dancing Bear," or "May there always be Mama." On the other hand, 'Soviet children also sing:

> *We live in our native collective farm in friendly,*
> *happy fashion.*
> *Together we sow, together we plow,*
> *Together we sing and dance.*

or

> *We are Lenin's grandchildren*
> *We are not yet Pioneers*
> *We are not yet Octobrists,*
> *But we know who we are for sure:*
> *We are Lenin's grandchildren!*
> *We are Lenin's grandchildren!*

Socialist morality is taught explicitly from a very young age. The young child is taught a few basic rules: "Don't throw toys; ask politely for a toy; don't grab it; put your toy back in place after playing with it." The child is also taught obedience and self-discipline, two vital underpinnings of the Soviet theory of child rearing.[1] However, most of this is done with a loving hand. In the nurseries and kindergartens which we visited in the Soviet Union we were particularly impressed by the warmth and loving quality of the nurses and teachers. There was a feeling of calm and cooperation in the child-rearing institutions we visited and a marked absence of tension.

This sense of calm and cooperation, the absence of overt dissension may be explained in part by a seeming lack of ambivalence on the part of the nurses and teachers both in China and in the Soviet Union. One feels that when a teacher in the Soviet Union or China says "no," there is no double message of "maybe" being transmitted. One senses a single-mindedness of belief and expectation of the child and a relaxed sureness on the part of the adults that is frequently not evident in our own society. And one does not sense the fear of children on the part of those who care for them in the Soviet Union or in China that one sometimes sees in the United States in mothers or mother-substitutes. Perhaps it is the fear of producing neurosis which is in the air so often between children and adults in our society.

One major difference noted immediately between the Soviet and the Chinese system is that the Soviet system is centralized and is therefore characterized by greater uniformity in its nurseries and kindergartens than in China, where the system is decentralized.

Decentralization is one of the major moves by the Chinese away from the Soviet model. The decision to decentralize much of the Chinese system of human services has stemmed from several factors: (1) The vastness and diversity of the Chinese population and the diffi-

[1] Kitty D. Weaver: *Lenin's Grandchildren* (New York: Simon and Schuster, 1971), p. 104.

culties of providing services under the close supervision of bureaucrats in Peking. (2) The strong Chinese belief in self-reliance, in "mobilizing the initiative of the people." (3) Their belief in tailoring services to meet the needs of various regions.

The Soviets, on the other hand, are characterized by a strong belief in credentialism. The Academy of Pedagogical Sciences, established in 1944, in conjunction with the Academy of Medical Science, has drawn up a detailed manual of instruction for pre-school programs which was published in 1962, revised in 1965 and again in 1969. There is a system of "methodists" and inspectors in each district to assure that the schools live up to the standards set for them. The methodists check on the qualifications of the teachers, give further training courses to older teachers, and arrange demonstrations and exhibits so that the teachers can keep up to date.

There is a stress in the Soviet pre-school system on qualifications and training that is not seen in the Chinese system since the Cultural Revolution. The director of a kindergarten must have an education from a teachers' college or a general education with special courses in teaching and at least two years of practical work in a kindergarten setting. The director of a yasli must have "higher-school special education." The music director must have special musical education, and kindergarten teachers must have either a two- or a three-year course at a pedagogical college.[2] By comparison, on the kibbutz, nurses are chosen from the kibbutz membership from among those women who wish to work with children and on the basis of personality qualifications. The nurses who work with infants have special

[2] Ibid., pp. 43–55.

training, sometimes in Israeli hospitals, and those who work with older children might attend an inter-kibbutz seminar in child psychology, educational theory, or common childhood problems. There are, in addition, frequent short courses that the nurses must attend. A nursery teacher must receive formal training before beginning her duties, two years' training at the teachers college.[3] Also, both on the kibbutz and in the Soviet Union, teachers of young children follow current educational and psychological thinking by keeping up with articles in journals which come to them regularly. This is in sharp contrast to the post-Cultural Revolution situation we saw in China, where there was no indication that teachers were keeping up with educational developments in other countries.

A kibbutz, or collective, is "an agricultural village in which all property, with minor exceptions, is collectively owned, in which work is collectively organized, and in which living arrangements—including the rearing of children—are, to a great degree, collective." [4] The history of the kibbutz movement goes back to the early 1920's, although there were collectives in Palestine as early as 1909, when young people, primarily in their late teens or early twenties, most of whom came from Poland, immigrated to Palestine from the ghettos of Eastern Europe. The anti-Semitism rampant in Eastern Europe, the narrow ghetto with its tight-knit paternalistic Jewish family, the traditional Jewish oppression of the female, and the anti-urban, pro-labor youth movement popular in the early 1900's all contributed

[3] Melford E. Spiro: *Children of the Kibbutz* (New York: Schocken Books, 1965), pp. 28–29.
[4] Spiro: *Kibbutz: Venture in Utopia* (New York: Schocken Books, 1970), p. 4.

to the move on the part of these young people from Eastern Europe to Palestine. Thus, a group of middle-class urbanites attempted to start a new rural life based on manual labor and collective living. By 1964 the kibbutz movement had grown to encompass approximately eighty thousand people living in two hundred and fifty kibbutzim but comprising only about 4 percent of the population of Israel.[5]

Between the early 1950's when Melford E. Spiro did his well-known study of the kibbutz that he called "Kiryat Yedidim" and the mid-1960's when Bruno Bettelheim studied a kibbutz that he called "Atid," the kibbutz movement had undergone many changes. These changes have increased in the last few years with the impact of the Six-Day War in 1967 and general pressures from outside the kibbutzim. However, there are many premises which the originators of the kibbutz movement held which are held, at least in part, today.

It is generally agreed that children should be raised collectively in peer groups by adults other than their parents, called "metapelets," in order to diminish the importance of the family, to free the woman from her traditional oppression, and to free the parent-child relationship from its traditional conflict. There is, of course, considerable variation in the systems used in various kibbutzim—for example, in some kibbutzim the children spend only the daytime in the nursery and spend the night with their parents, whereas in many others they spend twenty-four hours a day in the nursery, with only two-hour visits by their parents. There are kibbutzim in which the parents are not allowed to put their children to bed; there are kibbutzim in which

[5] Bettelheim, p. 29.

putting one's children to bed is a very important part of the day.

Generally, at the age of four or five days, the infant is brought to the nursery where he will be cared for twenty-four hours a day by the metapelet, except for feeding times, when he is nursed by his mother. Babies are weaned at from six to eight months, and the baby is first allowed in the parents' home at the age of six months. The babies remain in the infants' house from four days to one year, when the first major change in their lives occurs. At one year they are moved to the toddlers' house, where they must acclimate to new nurses as well as a new physical environment. It is in the toddlers' house, from the ages of fifteen to eighteen months, that the young child is collectively toilet-trained in much the same manner as in China—that is, put on the potty at regular times with the other children. The children remain in the toddlers' house from one year to roughly four years and are then moved to the kindergarten, where they remain until they are nearly six. At six they enter a transitional class, before going into primary school at age seven.

The daily routine in the toddlers' house is very similar to the daily routine in a Chinese kindergarten. One marked difference is that the children have time for a great deal of unsupervised play, particularly when they are in their collective playpens. The metapelets have housekeeping chores and leave the children to their own devices during that time. If some of the children cry for long periods, someone would go in to see what is wrong. It was during this time that Spiro observed a great deal of aggression among the children. He reports hitting as the most frequent type of aggression observed but also reports "hitting with an object, kicking, biting, pushing, throwing an object at the victim, destroying another's property, scratching, gouging, hair-pulling, pushing, smearing, choking, interfering with activity, hair-cutting, and penis pulling." [6] He felt that most acts of physical aggression were not instigated by any outward event—that is, they were caused by inner feelings rather than by the outer situation. He also stresses that the nurse was generally not present during these periods of play in which the aggression occurs.

At no time in China did we notice children of this age left unattended for long periods of time in the nursery or kindergarten. Furthermore, since acts of aggression by children at any age seemed so infrequent, we doubt that acts of aggression by children are allowed to go unchecked. These varying methods of handling aggression would be a fundamental difference in the upbringing of children in the kibbutz and the upbringing of children as we observed and discussed it in China. Part of the reason for this difference might stem from acceptance on the part of those who live in the kibbutz of Freudian psychology and of aggression as a natural component of man, possibly one which is better acted out than repressed. The Chinese, of course, do not study Freud and those who are aware of his teachings do not believe they are relevant to their setting. That the Chinese do not believe that aggression is necessarily inevitable seems evident.

Another fundamental difference between Chinese and kibbutz child-rearing practices involves the amount of direct verbal teaching which occurs. The Chinese accompany child-rearing with quotes from Mao on how children should relate to one another. This is in addi-

[6] Spiro: *Children of the Kibbutz,* p. 165.

tion to the collective physical setting, the implicit attitudes of the nurses, the sharing of equipment and toys, the daily routine, and the other facets of life which indicate to the small child how he is to behave and feel. In the kibbutz the nurses seem, at least with small children, to rely almost entirely on dealing with everyday situations and to use verbal expressions of idealized behavior less frequently than the Chinese. On the other hand, the nurses do encourage the children to share and to help each other. Four-year-olds may be seen helping each other to dress, sharing candy with each other, helping each other up when they fall and interfering when two other children are fighting. This was noted to occur at the instigation of the nurse far more often than as a spontaneous act.

There are many basic principles shared by people in the Soviet Union, Israel, and China which have a substantial influence on child-rearing. These principles are also held in common by other socialist countries, for socialism is the strain that is common to all three movements, even though each considers his a distinctive brand of socialism. Of the many premises which these three national groups hold in common, I would like to discuss four: their view of man, the focus on labor, the role of the individual and the individual's role in the group, and the role of women.

In each of the three societies there is a strain running through the talking and writing which indicates a fundamental belief in the perfectability of man. This has been mentioned earlier in relation to Mao's view that man can be taught and molded to reach higher levels, that there is, in fact, no goal too lofty even for the common peasant if he is given enough "education and re-education." This is a basic theme of Chinese society today; it is the basis of the May 7 schools to which intellectuals and bureaucrats thought guilty of revisionism are sent in order to "remold their world outlook"; it is basic tenet of the teacher's approach to "naughty children."

Anton Semonovich Makarenko, an educator whose work, *A Book for Parents,* has been read and reread in the Soviet Union by teachers and parents since the 1930's, when it was first published, says: "The profound meaning of educational work, and particularly the work of the family collective, consists in the selection and training of human needs, in bringing them to that high moral sense which is possible only in the classless struggle and which alone can urge on man to struggle for further perfection." [7] The underlying theme in much Soviet writing about child-rearing is that once a non-exploitative society has been promulgated, man can then, with training, teaching, and vigilance, become the kind, cooperative, responsible member of society which he is capable of becoming.

A group of parents on a kibbutz in the early 1950's were asked to rank in order of importance the values that they hoped would be inculcated in their children by collective education. The values ranked as follows: (1) work, (2) love of humanity, (3) responsibility to kibbutz, (4) good character, (5) intellectualism, (6) socialism, (7) Zionism, (8) social participation, (9) patriotism, (10) cooperation, (11) initiative, (12) good manners, (13) respect for parents. [8] This exalted list clearly indicates a belief on the part of kibbutz dwellers that human nature can be improved by education and a

[7] A. S. Makarenko: *A Book for Parents* (Moscow: Foreign Languages Publishing House, 1954), p. 41.
[8] Spiro: *Children of the Kibbutz,* pp. 20–21.

change of the environment in which people grow up. The kind of person envisioned by the educational directors of the Kibbutz Federation is one ". . . possessed of an ideological-political backbone on the one hand, and of a highly technical-vocational level on the other; who strives for a maximal combination of spiritual and physical labor . . . a person of deep and embracing culture, who will be capable of contributing to the ideational, economic, and cultural elevation of kibbutz society." [9] Thus, all three societies share the view that man has enormous potential for change and for developing noble motivation and behavior through education.

All three societies also share a belief in the value of manual labor and a commitment to integrating manual and intellectual labor. We have already discussed this aim in China with regard to the post-Liberation goals, the Cultural Revolution, and the training of children in nurseries and particularly in kindergartens. The same focus is to be found in the pre-school institutions in the Soviet Union. As in the Chinese nursery, learning to take care of yourself in the yasli is the first form of work. The two-year-old must learn to feed himself and to dress himself, and then he learns to wash dolls' clothes and clean and repair toys. The kindergarten children, particularly the older ones of five and six, have regular work activities such as setting and clearing the table, taking care of animals and plants, putting toys away, planting and growing vegetables, and cleaning up the yard.[10]

On the kibbutz Spiro studied, the kindergarten children bring food from the kitchen, clear the tables, empty the garbage, tend their own vegetable garden,

[9] Ibid., pp. 21–22.
[10] Weaver, pp. 112–22.

and care for a few animals. They eat the produce they grow, and the income from their poultry, goats, and sheep is applied to their group's needs.[11]

The third value held in common by all three societies is the importance of the group and the individual's responsibility to the group. Spiro found in Kiryat Yedidim the expectation that "the individual's motivations will always be directed to the promotion of the group's interests, as well as of his own." "Behavior is expected to be characterized by 'Ezra Hadidit' or mutual aid."[12] This concept of "mutual aid" is of course reminiscent of Mao's maxim "To love each other, help and care for each other." The kibbutz was an attempt to create an "organic community," a "chevra," or what can be compared to a commune in China, in which individual action must be decided upon in light of the effect it will have on the entire community. "Careerism," being concerned with getting ahead in one's own field without primary consideration for the needs of the group, was a great concern of the kibbutzim, since "doing your own thing" might be in direct opposition to the needs of the kibbutz and is an expression of the pursuit of individualism as much frowned upon in China today as in the kibbutz fifteen to twenty years ago. In a postscript written by Leslie Y. Rabkin and Melford E. Spiro to Spiro's study of Kiryat Yedidim, careerism was found to be less of a concern in 1970 on the kibbutz; individuals were freer to pursue their own particular interests than when Spiro had first studied the kibbutz.

Although there seems to be far more latitude to express one's individuality in the Soviet Union than in

[11] Spiro: *Children of the Kibbutz*, p. 210.
[12] Spiro: *Kibbutz: Venture in Utopia*, p. 30.

China, where the effort is very great, at the moment, to avoid careerism, the Soviet citizen is nevertheless considered a member of the collective. According to one source, "the children of the collectives should always regard themselves as part of Soviet society." Thus, as in China and in Israel, the child is taught that he is part of his family group, part of his collective, and part of the entire society as well.

According to Bettleheim, in his book *The Children of the Dream:* "The essential female role in the ghetto was one in which the woman's entire life was swept up in caring for husband and children, and nothing else." [13] It was this very role that the kibbutz men and women were trying to avoid in the organization of the kibbutz with its collective education. They were attempting to free women from the domestic role and to open up possibility of equality with men through equality of work. This value was surely held in common with the Soviet Union, which made an immediate commitment to equal rights for women and then attempted to fulfill that commitment by providing jobs, maternity leave, and an intricate system of public day care.

The Soviet commitment to equality for women is spelled out most clearly in the 1936 Constitution of the U.S.S.R., Article 122.

> Women in the U.S.S.R. are accorded equal rights with men in all spheres of economic, state, cultural, social, and political life.
> The possibility of exercising these rights is ensured to women by granting them an equal right with men to work, payment for work, rest and leisure, social in-

[13] Bettelheim, p. 45.

surance, and education, by state protection of the interests of mother and child, by state aid to mothers of large families and unmarried mothers, pre-maternity and maternity leave with full pay, and the provision of a wide network of maternity homes, nurseries, and kindergartens.[14]

Although women in the Soviet Union have made incredible progress toward equality, particularly in such fields as medicine and education, they are heavily burdened with housework and child-rearing in addition to tiring jobs. Nor have the women in Israel solved the problem of the role of women. In a recent article in the *American Journal of Orthopsychiatry*,[15] Menachem Gerson, the head of the Institute of Research on Kibbutz Education, points out that kibbutz-born women are both "dissatisfied and disillusioned" with their role in the kibbutz. They are less active in the administration of the kibbutzim; marriage and family "form the center of their lives," rather than work. Again, it must be stressed that people living on the kibbutzim in Israel comprise only 4 percent of the population, and the life style and goals of the rest of the country, which are often diametrically opposed to those of the kibbutz, are constantly impinging on the kibbutz residents.

In summary, there is a basic agreement of belief and purpose on the part of the nurses and teachers within institutions in China and the Soviet Union and on a kibbutz; they reinforce each other rather than conflict. Therefore, instead of getting multiple messages, the

[14] *The Woman Question: Selections from the Writings of Karl Marx, Frederick Engels, V. I. Lenin, Joseph Stalin* (New York: International Publishers, 1951), p. 48.
[15] Menachem Gerson: "Women in the Kibbutz," *American Journal of Orthopsychiatry*, Vol. 41, No. 4 (July 1971), pp. 566–73.

child gets basically one, even if from multiple people. I do not mean to overstate this consensus. There are obviously differences between people, but compared to the variety of values and attitudes found in the United States, the differences are minimal. This consensus among those who care for children is only reflective of the general consensus in the larger society of all three countries. Bettleheim, in describing kibbutz life, calls it a "society of high consensus where everyone sees the central issues of life more or less alike, and where everyone is under continuous scrutiny by nearly everyone else. Nothing can stay hidden. Asocial tendencies evoke immediate counter reactions, and these are usually enough to induce their repression." [16] This description of kibbutz life could as well be a description of Soviet or Chinese life.

[16] Bettelheim, p. 66.

9

"The Concern of One Generation for the Next"

Reach the ninth heaven high to embrace the
    moon
Or the five oceans deep to capture a turtle: ei-
    ther is possible.
    Return to merriment and triumphant songs.
    Under this heaven nothing is difficult,
    If only there is the will to ascend.

MAO TSE-TUNG
"Chingkangshan Revisited," 1965

9

The Concern of
One Generation
for the Next

THERE IS NO DOUBT THAT THE CHINESE HERI-
tage and culture are very different from those of the
United States. However, certain principles in the delivery of human services, techniques of child care, aspects
of the liberation of women, and basic principles which
underlie present Chinese society might well have some
applicability to our own society.

It must be stressed that the organization of Chinese
society is in a process of evolution; what we saw was
simply a moment in time. In the fall of 1971 the country was still recovering from the Cultural Revolution
and was just settling down to the reorganization of its
basic institutions. While all segments of the society had
been reorganized according to anti-elitist principles, it
was difficult to assess the permanence of the reorganization. The emphasis on Mao was still very much in evidence and his writings were of supreme importance in
teaching the values of the society. One saw evidence, as
well, of a "left dogmatism," as William Hinton described it in a public lecture in New York in the winter
of 1972, a mouthing of words and slogans without the
meaning necessarily always being in the forefront. Hinton cited examples of people being praised for the
number of Mao's quotations they had memorized
rather than for the way they had put them into prac-

tice. "All public, no self" has been the motto since the mid-1960's. Hinton hopes it will be increasingly replaced by "Public first, self second," a more realistic and lasting approach which takes into consideration the needs of society as well as the needs of the individual.

The possibility of mouthing the words rather than understanding and putting them into practice is most obvious in the nurseries and kindergartens, where the fine line between teaching a system of thought and merely teaching a liturgy becomes vividly apparent. Hearing children in several kindergartens singing the same political songs with the same gestures and expressions can be unnerving to the Western visitor; but the hope that a system of values is thus being transmitted is a reassuring one. The Chinese are the first to say that life is always a "struggle between two lines," and one hopes that the emphasis on those who memorize the most quotations will give way to an even greater emphasis on those who try to put them into practice.

One of the most striking aspects of the Chinese experiment is the use of human resources. The disdain for credentialism, the discouragement of careerism, the belief that each person can be trained to do meaningful work within a relatively short period of time, the use of on-the-job training, and the "I think I can" attitude inspire one to return home and reexamine the premises on which training, particularly training for human services, is based in one's own country. The barefoot doctor with his three months of training, the Red Guard doctor and health worker with their ten days of training, and the nursery-school teacher with her six months of training are startling examples of the innovative uses of manpower. That people are trained just to the level needed to do a given job, thereby minimizing boredom, is in sharp contrast to most training in the United States.

In China the implications of this willingness to experiment with short periods of training are greatest for women, who still lag behind in professional spheres. Red Guard doctors were chosen from among "housewives," and there are reports coming back from other Westerners visiting China of factories being set up in neighborhoods by "housewives," women who are not otherwise working or who have not been trained in other fields. For it is clear that the extent of liberation of women in China is still dependent upon the opportunities for employment. Without employment, or the opportunity to do productive labor, the woman has neither an independent income nor the opportunity to develop her talents or serve the society.

This leads us, of course, to an examination of the meaning of liberation for women. Some views of the liberation of women are shared by people in China and in the West: both societies agree on the necessity of equal pay for equal work; both societies agree on the need for available employment for those women who wish to work; major segments of both societies agree on the woman's right to limit the number of her children in order to be free enough to engage in other pursuits. However, with the changing sexual mores and with the easy availability of contraception, the women's liberation movement in the West has taken on the distinct flavor of sexual freedom as well. Liberation in the United States increasingly includes a lack of inhibition, social or internal, regarding sexual display and sexual activity. In China, as we have seen, liberation is not interpreted in any way to mean sexual freedom. It is interpreted to mean economic freedom and political freedom, freedom from physical harm, freedom from working like a slave, freedom from one's mother-in-law, and freedom from having ten children, but distinctly not sexual freedom.

For women in China, liberation is thought of, too, as freedom from being treated primarily as a sexual object. I am reminded of a story that a friend of mine, a speech and hearing therapist, told me recently. Feeling that a physician with whom she was working did not understand some aspects of hearing loss, she offered to interpret audiograms to him and to discuss with him in greater detail some aspects of hearing loss. He replied oh, he knew all about it and that her hair looked very cute that day. This would not happen in China.

Directly related to being regarded and regarding oneself as a sexual object is consumerism. As long as consumerism and its supporting advertising are central factors in our economy, women will continue to be urged to be sex objects and status symbols. Consumerism is used both as a panacea for the boredom which can occur so readily when talents are being under-utilized and as a catalyst for our economy. The cycle is ready-made: not enough jobs, women at home, women bored, buy a new dress or a new detergent or a new dishwasher.

Chen Yuanchi, a Chinese actress who is married to an American and recently came to the United States to live, has said, "In order for a women to liberate herself, she must help to liberate the working class." One wonders how best to apply this to the United States; she is saying, in my view, that for any group to be freed from oppression, all groups must be freed from oppression. Other minority leaders have been pointing out that in order for any group in our society to be liberated—

blacks, Puerto Ricans, Mexican-Americans—the poor of all colors and backgrounds must be liberated. It is not merely through finding one's own salvation that one is free, but through the working out of political, economic, and interpersonal solutions which, in the long run, will help the entire society.

To put it in other terms, perhaps it is through service rather than acquisition that one can be free. Perhaps liberation comes not from acquiring greater status, income, power, and a larger piece of the consumer pie, but rather in finding new values and goals. The *Shorter Oxford English Dictionary* defines "liberate" as "to set free, set at liberty; to release from (something)." Thus it is a process of shaking off, of discarding, of loosening bonds, not of acquiring or taking on ready-made masculine values.

Some of the leaders of the women's liberation movement in the United States are trying to "liberate" men from their traditional stereotyped roles as well as women from theirs. In this way, women are taking the leadership in the reexamination of human roles. One thinks of China in the 1930's and 1940's when the Communists were attempting to free women from their traditional roles and encouraged these women to work and fight for the revolution for everyone. Perhaps the women's movement in this country as well can be a catalyst toward the reexamination of our values and the roles that all of us, men and women, play in society.

Although they have made astonishing progress on the liberation of women, the Chinese are the first to admit that they still have a long way to go. In a recent issue of *Peking Review*, an article entitled "Women's Liberation in China," by Soong Ching Ling (Madame Sun Yat-sen), says in part:

Today in our country there are people's communes in rural places where women receive less pay than men for equal work in production. In certain villages patriarchal ideas still have their effect. Proportionately, more boys than girls attend school. Parents need the girls to do household work. Some even feel that girls will eventually enter another family and therefore it would not pay to send them to school. Moreover, when girls are to be married, their parents often ask for a certain amount of money or various articles from the family of the would-be husband. Thus the freedom of marriage is affected. Finally, as farmers want to add [to] the labour force in their families, the birth of a son is expected, while that of a daughter is considered a disappointment. This repeated desire to have at least one son has an adverse effect on birth control and planned birth. A woman with many children around her naturally finds it too difficult to participate in any productive labor. Another thing hampering a working woman is her involvement in household work. This prevents many women from full, wholehearted participation in public services.[1]

It is clear that many of the pre-Liberation views still persist in the countryside in China. Comrade Soong goes on to say that "genuine equality between the sexes can be realized and the Women's Liberation Movement will be ended when and only when . . . the feudal-patriarchal and other exploiting-class ideologies are completely uprooted." [2] Thus, she is saying that women will be liberated when the old feudal-patriarchal ideas are finally gone, and also when no group is being exploited by another. This I think is the meaning of

[1] Ching Ling Soong: "Women's Liberation in China," *Peking Review*, Vol. 15, No. 6 (February 11, 1972), p. 7.
[2] Ibid., p. 7.

Chen Yuanchi's comment that women can be liberated only if they help liberate the working class. She is also saying that the struggle is between the old ideology and the new, rather than the personalized *ad hominem* struggle that much of the women's liberation movement has become in the United States. The individual male-female conflict aroused by the women's liberation movement in the United States is avoided in China, since the Chinese see the conflict as one between ideologies, not between individuals. An individual who impedes the liberation of women is viewed as the victim rather than the perpetrator of the old feudal ideology and the response is "reeducation" rather than hostility.

In the area of education, many issues are raised by the kind of pre-school education we saw in China. One of the most common questions I am asked is, "Doesn't the lack of individuality stifle creativity?" In our society, where creativity seems so closely linked to finding whatever is unique in each person, to ferreting out the occasional genius, to avoiding the standardization and conformity that occur when the group is emphasized over the individual, it may appear likely that the Chinese way will produce uniform, prescribed thinking and stifle unusual ability or insight.

Before we can adequately measure another society's creativity, we must define the word, because one society's creativity might well be another society's decadence. The Chinese today regard as creativity whatever furthers their cause in an innovative way. In the West we have a different view of the creative process. Should we measure creativity on their terms or on ours? Or should we use their terms to measure their creativity and our terms to measure ours? I think we shall have to wait another generation before evaluating the impact of Chinese society on its people's creativity, however it is defined.

In addition to viewing the Chinese individual as part of a group, part of a collective, with political thoughts prescribed by the Party, we must recognize that great numbers of Chinese citizens are imbued with a mission. The feeling which comes through most clearly and which we found most moving was this sense of mission, this sense of participation and commitment to an ideal greater than one's self. The group is clearly more important than the individual, and it is a group with spirit and dedication. When trying to evaluate the effect of collectivity on creativity, one must add in this dimension of spirit and commitment, for there is little question that it must have some effect on an individual's output. How long the Chinese can maintain this high degree of dedication, spirit, optimism—indeed, religious fervor—is a key question. The People's Republic is still a young government; many Chinese can still remember the "bitter past"; their original leaders are still with them. Whether these leaders have been able to imbue the population with their values and goals, codified in Mao's writings, sufficiently to carry on the revolutionary tradition after the leaders have gone remains to be seen.

This commitment to goals greater than one's self, this sense of mission that one sees in China today, raises relevant questions for those in the West concerned with the plight of young people whose despair, cynicism, and feeling of impotence are rampant. For whatever else the Chinese are teaching their children, they are teaching them that they can do something about famine, flood, the building of an enormous bridge or a canal, the Imperialist "paper tigers," lowering the birth rate, providing medical care, or running the schools. The Chinese are using and promoting "people power." As the Foolish Old Man said when he was scoffed at for trying to remove the mountain, "When I die, my sons will carry on; when they die, there will be my grandsons, and then their sons and grandsons, and so to infinity. High as they are, the mountains cannot grow any higher, and with every bit we dig, they will be that much lower. Why can't we clear them anyway?" This commitment to values larger than one's self in combination with the belief that with hard work and careful thought almost anything can be accomplished is a powerful tool in the raising of children.

Are there specific aspects of the Chinese pre-school system which might be helpful to us? I think there are. Certainly, maternity leave should be available to working women and might be financed jointly by the employer and the federal government. Too, the establishment of nursing rooms and nurseries in institutions of employment would facilitate the mother's return to work and provide economic, ethnic, and racial integration of the children. For example, children of doctors, nurses, nurse's aides, orderlies, cleaning and kitchen workers, technicians, and house staff would be attending the nursery in a hospital. Child-care centers might be supported by the employer, the federal government, and to some degree by the parents.

In a highly diverse society such as that of the United States, where goals, values, and educational philosophy are not for the most part held in common, mothers might well feel anxious about leaving their children at a young age with adults who might not share the mother's views of child-rearing. It is one thing to permit another woman to teach one's child to read; it is quite another for another woman to toilet-train him. Parental participation in the formation and administration of the nurseries would be extremely important in assuring that the institution was sensitive to the diverse needs of the children.

Finally, we might reevaluate our attitudes about child-rearing. Our understanding of the psychology of children has become highly sophisticated in the past thirty years and, due to the mass media, relevant concepts have been widely disseminated to the general public. Concepts such as ambivalence, sibling rivalry, Oedipal feelings, and the normalcy of aggression are commonplace, even if not referred to in technical terms. Freudian thinking has been popularized on television day and night. Now we expect love-hate relationships, we expect Johnny to have mixed feelings about his baby brother, we expect him to want to do away with his father, even if just in fantasy, and we expect anger and aggression. And, as any newspaper or news program tells us, we get it. Perhaps we have come full-circle. Perhaps now that we expect certain personality developments, our expectation creates their expression. Perhaps it is our anticipation of sibling rivalry which exacerbates its manifestation. The Chinese, in the handling of their children, seem to expect good behavior, cooperation, and obedience and, in general, get it. Although they clearly recognize that there is a non-cooperative, hostile, aggressive side to man, they do not emphasize it. They emphasize that side which they wish to promote. They emphasize the cooperative, not the competitive; the love, not the hate.

Bronfenbrenner, in his study of child-rearing in two countries, *Two Worlds of Childhood: U.S. and*

U.S.S.R., has proposed a criterion for judging the worth of a society: "the concern of one generation for the next." According to Bronfenbrenner: "If the children and youth of a nation are afforded opportunity to develop their capacity to the fullest, if they are given the knowledge to understand the world and the wisdom to change it, then the prospects for the future are bright. In contrast, a society which neglects its children, however well it may function in other respects, risks eventual disorganization and demise." [3] Bronfenbrenner explores "the concern of one generation for the next" in the Soviet Union and in the United States, and although he finds that in the Soviet Union children are more likely to be in day-care centers and kindergartens, and due to the long hours of working, shopping, and commuting, Soviet parents spend less time at home than American parents, he also finds that Soviet parents spend more time talking with their children and doing things with them than do American parents. He cites the ascendancy of television and the peer group as major influences on American children and raises the question whether permissiveness has become an abdication of the parental role. [4]

Everywhere in the Soviet Union the common expression is that children are the privileged class. It is a privilege not of material goods—although chances are they

[3] Urie Bronfenbrenner: *Two Worlds of Childhood: U.S. and U.S.S.R.* (New York: Russell Sage Foundation, 1970), p. 1.
[4] While the peer group is extremely important in the Soviet Union as well as in the United States, there is one vital difference: in the Soviet Union the peer group transmits and enforces the values decided upon by the larger society, whereas in the United States the peer group forms its own values, to some degree independently from the rest of society and often at odds with it.

eat better and have better medical care than the rest of the population—but a privilege born of the care and concern of the adults in the society. Mothering is shared in the Soviet Union; every woman seems to be every child's mother. On our first day in Leningrad, one of our sons was told by a woman to remove his feet from the rung of a table. It was "uncultured," she told him. Other times, employees in hotels in which we were staying would express concern as to whether our children were dressed warmly enough. Mothering is truly diffused throughout the society.

Although the cultural climate in China is very different from that in the Soviet Union, one still gets the feeling of a diffusion of responsibility for children; one woman would not hesitate to speak to another woman's child if she felt any need for doing so. The myth has grown up in the United States that the best mothering is one-to-one, or each mother caring for her own children. This belief is starting to be questioned from the point of view of the mother who is often angry, depressed, or bored at home, and from the point of view of the child who is not getting sufficient stimulation from other children and upon whom the burden of performance is great because through him the mother performs. The myth also exists that day care will break down family structure, will weaken the bonds of affection between parents and children and the feelings of responsibility for children on the part of parents. Although we have examined radically different ways of child-rearing, there seems to be no evidence that family structure is weakened, except in the case of Israel, where that was one of the goals, that children are any less loved by their parents, or that their psyches are damaged in any way by multiple or shared mothering.

On the contrary, Bronfenbrenner suggests that children in the Soviet Union are more adequately mothered than those in our country. Perhaps when a society thinks enough of its children to provide adequate day care, the children do not become the neglected people but rather the privileged people, as they are in the Soviet Union.

The West is clearly going through a time of major reassessment of the role of the woman. Along with this reassessment must come a reassessment of child-rearing practices, for in order for women to be free to pursue their own interests, to explore their potential, and to serve society, there must be alternative child-rearing patterns available. Many other societies have experimented with varying child-rearing modalities; it is imperative that we examine these techniques and evolve techniques that suit the needs of our society. The Chinese constantly say that they cannot export their form of revolution. So they cannot export their form of liberation for women or their form of pre-school child care. What will liberate women in their society may not be meaningful in another society; the system that provides adequate care for children in China may not work elsewhere. But some of their principles may be useful in our society.

Like the Chinese, we must search out whatever in our past can enhance our future. We must find techniques which are consonant with our cultural heritage and mesh them with our goals for a future society. Only if we are open to change and willing to relate to each other in new ways can we assure the optimum development of each human being—man, woman, and child—and of our society.

Selected Reading List

For those who wish to explore further the issues raised in this book, the following may be helpful.

JACK BELDEN: *China Shakes the World*. New York: Monthly Review Press, 1949.

BRUNO BETTELHEIM: *The Children of the Dream*. New York: Avon, 1970.

URIE BRONFENBRENNER: *Two Worlds of Childhood: U.S. and U.S.S.R.* New York: Russell Sage Foundation, 1970.

WILLIAM BRUGGER: "The Male (and Female) in Chinese Society," *Impact of Science on Society*. UNESCO, Vol. XXI, No. 1 (1971).

JEROME CH'EN, ed.: *Mao*. Englewood Cliffs, N.J.: Prentice-Hall, Inc., 1969.

COMMITTEE OF CONCERNED ASIAN SCHOLARS: *China! Inside the People's Republic*. New York: Bantam Books, 1972.

MICHAEL B. FROLIC: "What the Cultural Revolution Was All About," *The New York Times Magazine,* October 24, 1971.

FELIX GREENE: *China*. New York: Ballantine Books, 1962.

HAN SUYIN: *A Mortal Flower*. New York: Putnam, 1966.

————: *The Crippled Tree*. New York: Putnam, 1965.

————: "Reflections on Social Change," *Bulletin of the Atomic Scientists*. Vol. 22, No. 6 (June 1966).

William Hinton: *Fanshen*. New York: Vintage Books, 1966.

K. S. Karol: *China: The Other Communism*. New York: Hill and Wang, 1968.

A. S. Makarenko: *A Book for Parents*. Moscow: Foreign Language Publishing House, 1954.

Jan Myrdal: *Report from a Chinese Village*. New York: New American Library, 1966.

Victor Nee: *The Cultural Revolution at Peking University*. New York: Monthly Review Press, 1969.

Joan Robinson: *The Cultural Revolution in China*. Baltimore, Md.: Penguin Books, 1969.

Myra Roper: *China: The Surprising Country*. New York: Doubleday, 1966.

Edgar Snow: *Red China Today*. New York: Vintage Books, 1971.

Melford E. Spiro: *Children of the Kibbutz*. New York: Schocken Books, 1965.

————: *Kibbutz: Venture in Utopia*. New York: Schocken Books, 1970.

Kitty D. Weaver: *Lenin's Grandchildren*. New York: Simon and Schuster, 1971.

C. K. Yang: *Chinese Communist Society: The Family and the Village*. Cambridge, Mass.: M.I.T. Press, 1965.

A Sample Kindergarten Reader

TITLE: To Carry Out the Revolutionary Line of Chairman Mao Despite Hardships and Difficulties. Advanced Achievements of Comrade Han Yu-fen

> *The experience of history is worthwhile. One line, one point of view must be discussed often and repeatedly. To discuss with a small minority is not enough. We must let the broad revolutionary masses know also.*
>
> *Our team works for the liberation of the people and for the benefit of the people.*

MAO TSE-TUNG

Compiled by the Committee of the People's Liberation Army Air Force stationed in Shanghai. Published by the People's Press of Shanghai.

Han Yu-fen came from a poor family in Heilungkiang Province. The evil old society had caused the death of her father. When she was nine years old, she was forced to serve as a maid at the landlord's household. During the winter she was forced to go barefoot to the well to draw water. She bled when her skin and flesh were cut by ice. Therefore, she developed deep hatred for landlords as a class and determined to avenge this injustice.

The spring thunder struck, the poor saw the red sun. After the thirteen-year-old Han was liberated, she hurried to the barracks of the People's Army. Pointing to the scars on her body, she accused the exploitative class. She told the comrades: Chairman Mao's troops liberated me; I want to join the troops of Chairman Mao, follow the Communist Party in annihilating the man-eating wolves.

After Han had joined the army, she was assigned to a field hospital as a medic. With the assistance of the party and comrades, she learned quickly. "To gain the world for the poor, we must follow Chairman Mao," she began to realize. Although she was young and physically weak, she was eager to pursue every task. After the first year she was rated a "first-class model medic." . . .

"To serve the people" is the road pointed out by Chairman Mao. It is the pathway toward practice in defending the Chairman's revolutionary line. To direct her own activities, Han used the brilliant thought "to serve the people." In order to elevate the quality of service rendered to the people, she practiced giving herself injections without light and mastered the true ability of safeguarding the combat readiness of the troops. . . .

"To serve the people is to emulate Comrade Norman Bethune." Once Han received a telephone call about a peasant woman who had been suffering postpartum hemorrhage for three days and nights and who had to have emergency treatment. In heavy snow, Han rushed over to the patient's home. Meanwhile, a bad doctor had already suggested that preparations be made for the funeral. Han would have none of that. She persisted in the treatment for over seventy minutes and finally resuscitated the patient. . . .

Han made it her primary responsibility to defend Chairman Mao's revolutionary line. Since the beginning of the Great Proletarian Cultural Revolution, she joined the masses and opened fire on the rebellious, treasonous, anti-revolutionary revisionist clique of Liu Shao-chi. They enthusiastically espoused Chairman Mao's revolutionary line. . . .

Han followed every line of Chairman Mao's instruction, adhered closely to his great strategy. After Chairman Mao had issued the latest directive that the cadres should join in manual labor in the countryside, she, with "quotations from Chairman Mao" in her hand and a small medical kit on her back, joined the third engineering squad and began the health and sanitation work. . . .

Due to Han's great understanding of the comrades' mental and physical state, she did a good job of providing health care for the squad. The sick comrades did not need to go to her for medical care; she herself went directly to the sick and ministered to them. At the same time, she encouraged the sick to be determined in fighting their illness. The comrades were moved to say that Dr. Han's dedication in bringing help to the patient is quite unique. . . .

Han insisted on laboring and fighting together with other comrades. Whenever emergency maintenance work had to be done in the night, she hurried to the air base to assist the workers by providing light. People were so moved that they came to look upon her as an example to be followed. Han sincerely replied to them: "You, comrades, are all my good teachers. Receiving my reeducation from you, comrades, is the major lesson I have had in coming to this squad.". . .

She studied Chairman Mao's teaching with new personnel in health care and enthusiastically aided them in learning from practice. This follows Chairman Mao's teaching that we should learn "war from war." She let the internes practice injections on her own children. . . .

Due to the necessity of preparing for war, the air base sent her to a hospital in Shanghai to further her studies. There, witnessing the tremendous revolutionary atmosphere in the hospital, she was inspired to tell the workers: "In order to defend Chairman Mao's revolutionary line, please assign me often to the most difficult tasks.". . .

Han followed step by step the revolutionary line of Chairman Mao. Also, she zealously assisted the proletariat brothers and sisters to travel on Chairman Mao's revolutionary road. The chief of the operating room had a negative attitude toward the patients. Han went through the "remember the bitter past and contemplate the present goodness" process with her and helped engrave the motto "To serve the people" deep in the chief's heart. . . .

There was a patient with phlebitis whose left leg developed serious gangrene. After the "specialists" in the hospital had determined the case incurable except by "proximal amputation," Han thought of Chairman Mao's teaching: "Resuscitate the dead and heal the wounded, practice revolutionary humanitarianism." She was determined to preserve the leg that had been "sentenced to death by the capitalistic line for health and sanitation."

Han was determined to administer an integrated Chinese-Western medical treatment for the patient with phlebitis. In order to learn the prescriptions among the people, she used her day off, after night duty, to go to a commune ten miles away to consult the "peasant doctor." Han went along with the peasant doctor to collect medicinal herbs. She said, "For the benefit of the people, we must beat out new paths with Mao Tse-tung thought." . . .

During the course of treatment, some doctors began to waver. According to published literature, phlebitis was hard to cure. Han said, "We must consider the future of the patient. We should not take the alternative route in the face of difficulty. We ought to be firm in carrying out Chairman's Mao's revolutionary line."

Han often studied Chairman Mao's teachings with the patient. She inspired in the patient the confidence of victory over disease for the sake of revolution. Under the leadership of the hospital, and with the active support of the masses and the close cooperation of the patient, the gangrenous leg was finally cured, after Han's careful treatment. She heralded another triumphant song for Chairman Mao's revolutionary line.

The hospital had admitted a woman teacher with recurrent cancer. A lot of consulting doctors said, "Advanced stage of cancer cannot be cured." On the one hand, Han encouraged the patient to have the confidence of victory over disease. On the other hand, she was determined that even with odds of one in a hundred, she would fight for that one percent and think of ways to save the life of this class sister. . . .

From the Workers Propaganda Team members to doctors and nurses, from auxiliary personnel to drivers and cooks, everybody actively supported the war on the tumor. Letters expressing determination and letters of suggestions arrived at the hospital's revolutionary committee. The wisdom and warmth of the masses profoundly educated Han. . . .

Following the direction of the revolutionary lines of Chairman Mao, the hospital successfully removed the malignant tumor which previously no one had dared to touch. They achieved a great victory in the "war of annihilating the capitalist and promoting the proletariat." The good news was learned, the hospital resounded with cheers and cries of "Long live Chairman Mao!" Han, together with the revolutionary masses walking the revolutionary road of Chairman Mao, continued forward.

Index